Jasper

xl

MW01223169

RETHINKING EDUCATION

Learning and the New Renaissance

Stephen Murgatroyd, PhD FBPsS FRSA
Chief Scout, The Innovation Expedition

A FutureThink Press Book

The rights of Stephen Murgatroyd to be identified as the author of this work have been asserted according to the US Copyright, Designs and Patent Act of 1988 and appropriate Canadian copyright law.

Printed in the United States of America.

Murgatroyd, Stephen 1950-

Rethinking Innovation – Learning and the New Renaissance

ISBN: 978-1-105-09422-4

If the ideas outlined here of interest, then you can read more at www.renaissanceleaders.org

First printing in October 2011

This Book is Dedicated to the late and much missed

Chris Gonnet, Superintendent of Schools, Grande Prairie Public Schools, Alberta, Canada - an inspiration and a friend.

And also to

JC Couture, Phil McCrae, Michael Podlosky, Carol Henderson, Hon. Dave Hancock, Spence Nichol, Andy Hargreaves, Dennis Shirley, Pasi Sahlberg and all of the teachers and school administrators in Grande Prairie, Livingstone Range, and the members of the Alberta Teachers' Association who are committed to educational transformation and have enjoined the journey to change.

With thanks to
Nadine Riopel and Susan Wasson

Foreword

Co-Creating a Learning Alberta

This publication represents the first of a series of books that will profile some of the forward thinking work being undertaken by leading education researchers and policy experts focused on transforming the face of public education and the future of Alberta. The *Co-creating a Learning Alberta* book series is a partnership with leading public policy thinkers and the Alberta Teachers' Association that flows from the public lecture series called *"Learning our Way to the Next Alberta."* Since its inception in 2004, this lecture series has drawn over 5,000 participants and continues to push our thinking about the hopes and possibilities for the future of this province and is profiled at *www.learningourway.ca* .

In these public lectures, three questions have come to dominate the conversations about the future of the Alberta: *What is the Alberta that the world needs to see? What kind of Albertans do we need to become to get us there?* and *How will leadership in learning help us become our best selves?* As with the lecture series, this book provides important insights about the possibilities facing our schools as Alberta sits on the edge of taking on a true leadership role as a global hub of ingenuity and innovation.

The challenge put forward by Stephen Murgatroyd for public education is for citizens and educators to engage in a courageous conversation about the central role for educational development as a lever for creating the Alberta we desire for the decades ahead, though the scope of the book goes beyond Alberta. This is not an easy challenge. Alberta's student population is expected to increase by 100,000 (from 600,000) before the end of the decade, bringing growing diversity and complexity to our school communities. Currently, Calgary's thriving economy makes it home to more immigrants per capita than Montreal – nearly a quarter of the population is a visible minority. Yet, along with the vibrancy and hope that growth brings, so too comes distractions and obstacles to progress. For example, as Murgatroyd outlines, for too long the basic education system has been held back by a managerial accountability model that limits the capacity of schools and teachers and diminishes professional responsibility of educators. As well, misdirected learning technology policies that ignore the teaching and learning contexts of Alberta schools have not been helpful. In both cases, Murgatroyd moves beyond critique to offering possibilities for positive change. Drawing on research partnerships with the Alberta Teachers' Association, Murgatroyd outlines thoughtful ideas that will support informed transformation and sustainable school development.

I look forward to the public dialogue that this first publication of the *Co-Creating a Learning Alberta* book series will help create.

Gordon Thomas
Executive Secretary
Alberta Teachers' Association
October 2011

Preface

In 1972 I began teaching at Fairwater School, Cwmbran in South Wales[1] while at the same time researching counselling in schools, truancy and school effectiveness with Professor David Reynolds[2]. Since then I have been involved passionately in educational reform and development activities, writing about this work in the journal *School Organization*[3] and publishing chapters, books and papers seeking to encourage and enable developments in school leadership. The work involved significant work in Wales, Ireland and England, often in partnership with others, most especially Dr. Colin Morgan[4].

In 1986, on my arrival in Canada, my first major task was to develop, with Noreen O'Hare of the Alberta Teachers' Association, a substantial leadership program for aspiring and practising principals of schools. Many of the participants in this program (which spanned a five year period to 1991 and involved some 200 persons) remain friends and colleagues.

When I was a Vice President at Axia NetMedia (1998-2003) I had market responsibility for the partnership between our firm and the Galileo Educational Network[5], based in Calgary. This inspirational group, led by the late Pat Clifford, Sharon Friesen (now Associate Dean at the University of Calgary) and Brenda Gladstone, does pioneering work with teachers in the transformation of teaching and learning and are true pioneers of innovative thinking and practice. I was later Chair of the Board of Galileo – a service I was honoured to perform.

Since 2007 I have again been working with the Alberta Teachers' Association on the development of new ways of thinking about schooling, new forms of accountability, and new models of learning. Key to this work has been the genuine and meaningful involvement of Andy Hargreaves, JC Couture, Pasi Sahlberg, Dennis Shirley, Phil McRae, Michael Podlosky, and ATA President Carol Henderson. I should make clear that the inspiration for this work is the pioneering work teachers do each day in classrooms and the terrific leadership shown by all levels of school administrators. I should also make clear that this book is in no way sanctioned by the ATA.

One close colleague in this work was Chris Gonnet, Superintendent for Grande Prairie Public Schools in northern Alberta. Chris was a friend, coach, colleague and mentor and also an inspiration. His sudden and unexpected death early in 2011 was a loss to me and, more importantly, to all who care about education in Alberta. He is missed, but his inspiration is one reason this book exists.

This work has taken me to workshops and conferences in the United States, Sweden, Britain, Finland, Ireland and many other places. I am especially grateful to the Catholic Archdiocese of Philadelphia for its encouragement of my work and the invitation it has extended to me to work with its elementary and high school leadership teams.

As a lifelong advocate of quality public education, a former teacher and someone directly engaged with school reform, there is a great deal of turbulence at this time. As you will see in Chapter One, this is part of the transitional phase the world is going through from one age to another – an "in between time".

educational ecotone

While this is messy and involves a great deal of uncertainty, it is also a great time to experiment, explore and examine opportunities.

The Innovation Expedition, of which I am a part, has been doing this in a systematic way since 1991 when it was founded at the Banff Centre by Donald Simpson. More recently, we have been describing this current period as a new renaissance – a period which has many features and similarities which parallel the medieval renaissance, which was also a period of major transition.

In our thinking on renaissance leadership, published in a book of this same name[6], we outlined why we thought this renaissance was occurring and what renaissance leadership looked like. In this book, I extend this to education (see Chapter 8). It also calls for new forms of governance (Chapter 9) and new forms of accountability (Chapter 7). Most critical of all, it requires a refocusing of the work of the school (Chapters 1 and 2), new thinking about learning (Chapter 3) and teaching (Chapter 4) and new approaches to leveraging technology (Chapter 5), with an emphasis on giving the learner choice for a mindful and meaningful education (Chapter 6).

expanding the edge (handwritten)

To some, this may seem a radical agenda. To others, overly tame. The point of the book is to provide a basis for dialogue and conversation – a challenge dialogue for the future of schooling, something we actually started as part of the partnership between Finland and Alberta. If you live and work in Alberta, you can join in a debate about this work by going to http://www.learningourway.ca/index.php/forum and signing in, or you sign the petition at http://www.gopetition.com/petition/35101.html. While both of these web based resources are focused on Alberta, my home, they have a wider significance.

The overarching theme of the book is the need for a transformation of learning and teaching and the redesign of the school in line with an understanding of why this is required, given the 21st century renaissance we are living through. This renaissance is described to some extent in Chapter 1, but is the focus of the final chapter of this book (Chapter 10).
Let the journey continue!

Stephen Murgatroyd, PhD FBPsS FRSA
Canmore, Edmonton, Toronto October 2011

cross-pollination and education ecotone (handwritten margin note)

Chapter 1

The Need for Change In Education

Education in the developed world is at a tipping point. It is clear that an industrial model of education, which served the world well for many years, is undergoing major change and that those who lead educational systems, whether politicians, teacher leaders, concerned parents or students, want to see a "systems change" or educational "transformation". While there is general agreement that change is needed, this is where the agreement ends: few can agree what the changes should look like, how fast they can be made and what resources and supports are needed to sustain the changes to be made over time. In short: *we are stuck.*

Three Drivers for Change

Three things are driving the call for change. These are: (a) we could do better; (b) the demands of the new economy; and (c) the impact of technology on young people and society.

Let us introduce each of these change drivers in turn. Later, we will explore them in more depth.

We Can do Better

First, there is the general sense that we could do better. Every two years the Organization for Economic Cooperation and Development (OECD) conducts a review of educational systems using data collected from standardized tests taken by students in member countries' school systems. The results, known as PISA (Program for International Student Assessment), provide a league table of performance in three areas; reading; mathematics; and science. In the 2010 release of these data, the top six jurisdictions were Shanghai (a city), Finland, Hong Kong (a region), Singapore, Japan and Korea[7]. While their positions varied by discipline (Finland came second in science and sixth in mathematics, for example), these six jurisdictions dominate the league table; their educational systems consistently produce the best outcomes by the measures used. The US came twenty third in science, seventeenth in reading and didn't make the top twenty five in mathematics. Canada does well – eighth in science, sixth in reading and tenth in mathematics. However, all feel they could do better.

Most schools pay no attention to PISA tables or to the challenge they provide for Ministers of Education. They are focused on their performance – the successes and failures they experience in their work with students. Every teacher is proud of some of their achievements, but thinks that they can do better. They each have stories of students who have gone on from their classroom to do well, but will also happily describe those who should have done well, but didn't and those that didn't try. Teachers know that schools could do better.

The mantra "we can do better" is the major driver for change in education. Looking at just one system – that of Alberta, Canada (which sits just behind Finland in the PISA analysis of system performance) – this is a list of the areas in which all agree it "can do better":

- **Alberta has a high level of high school dropout**. The data on drop outs from high school are very clear - 11.3% of students drop out overall (tied for 2nd overall behind Manitoba), 9.9% in cities (3rd overall behind Manitoba and Quebec), 17% in small towns (1st overall among all provinces) and 21.7% in rural areas (1st overall among all provinces).

- **Alberta has the lowest high school to post-secondary transition rate of all provinces,** with only 48% of high school students going to post-secondary education within four years of leaving high school – the national average is 62%. Some 16% of those who attend college or university do not continue their studies after the end of their first year.

- **Literacy levels amongst those employed in Alberta are problematic** – a 2006 study of the workforce (2.1 million persons) suggests that some 850,00 employees (40% of those employed) have a level of functional literacy below that required for the positions they occupy.

- **Poor performance of First Nations and Métis students** - In the past three years, fewer than 15% of grade 9 students in First Nations band-operated schools and fewer than 50% of First Nations students in other school systems met the Acceptable Standard in mathematics, science and social studies. So serious were these issues that, in 2010, the Minister intervened in the Northlands School. Completion rates for aboriginal students in Alberta's post-secondary system are also low – 42% as compared to 60% for the non-aboriginal students who attend colleges and universities in Alberta. A report prepared for the Premier of Alberta in May of 2011 suggests that achieving parity for aboriginal Albertans in educational performance should be a major strategic priority for Alberta[8].

- **Significant erosion in support to students with special needs** – 41% of teachers report that, in 2009, services and support for special needs students declined in comparison to previous years[9].

- **Student engagement in learning levels are low** – A study by the Metiri Group (US) suggests that, on average, student engagement in their junior and senior high school work is less than 20%, with most behaving as tactically involved (51%), compliant (21%), withdrawn (5%) or defiant (3%). Data for Alberta from a number of Masters and doctoral studies shows this same pattern.

- **Teacher turnover remains a concern** – Average teacher turnover in Alberta is 38% over a four year period – just 62% of teachers remain in post four years after they began. Teaching (with the exception of those who teach students with special needs) is no longer a "top ten" Canadian job[10]. One third of new teachers express the view that they will leave the profession within five years of starting their first teaching position.

- **The quality of the education systems physical infrastructure is declining.** Each year the Government of Alberta assesses the fitness for use of Alberta school buildings, rating them on a simple scale from "good" to "poor" – since 2005, the number in the "fair" category has increased (from 25% to 29%) while the number in the "good" category has declined (from 73% to 67%)[11].

- **Technology adoption levels are modest** – Some 50% of Alberta school teachers use technology regularly and appropriately in their lessons [12], though recent research suggests that getting past this number will require significant investments in professional development and a freeing up of curriculum demands on teachers[13].

- **Employers are becoming less satisfied with the outcomes of Alberta's investments in education** – In the tri-annual survey of employer satisfaction with the graduates (including apprenticeship graduates) of the post-secondary system, satisfaction declined from 94% in 2005-6 to 88% in 2007-8[14].

While this may sound bleak, Alberta is a high performing school jurisdiction according to the PISA analysis – in the top ten in the world and the leader within Canadian provincial systems. It is also one of the wealthiest economies per capita in the world (GDP per capita is $82,302US compared with the Canadian average of $45,000US) [15], mainly because it has an abundant supply of energy and natural resources. But it can do better. This is why the transformation of the school system is a major agenda item in Alberta.

The New Economy

The second driver is the new economy. Driven in part by technology and in part by globalization, the new economy is intensely focused on knowledge.

In Kenya, which has become a leading supplier of cut flowers to the world, cell phones are used to manage the traceability of goods. Flower stems are fitted with RFID chips which enable anyone at any stage in the supply chain to know where the flower was grown, what soil conditions and fertilizers were used, when it was cut, how it was shipped and key dates in its journey. This information is used to determine the quality of the flower and its "freshness" on arrival at its final destination. In the forest industry, it is now possible to assess the value of a stand of trees in a forest using satellite data and machine intelligence so that sustainable harvesting plans can be developed which link the value of fibre cut to its potential uses, not just as lumber or the raw ingredient for pulp and paper manufacture, but in terms of the value of the tree for other products; bio-chemicals; bioenergy; bioplastics; biofuels; and so on.

Knowledge is key to decision making and to the work of business. It is also key to non-profits, the functioning of government and civil society. We have moved from a knowledge-poor economy to a knowledge-rich economy, with a requirement that those who serve that economy need to have substantial knowledge on entry, and engage as life-long learners so as to maintain their knowledge-readiness throughout their economic service, either as workers or as citizens. The general concern is that many citizens and workers do not have the knowledge and skills to be successful in the twenty first century. The specific concern is that the creativity and design skills so critical to this new economy are missing in many of those who graduate from different levels of schooling.

This shift from a Tayloristic economy where workers were told what to do minute by minute and work was repetitive and functional, to an economy where creativity, imagination and problem solving are critical components of many workers daily routines is a major change. It carries the implication that more and more of those in the workforce need a high level of knowledge and skill so as to perform their work well. In Ontario, Canada's largest province, the government has set a target that 70% of the working population should hold a post-secondary qualification (a college or university qualification) by 2020. It has set this target in order to retain a position as a competitive economy in a growingly knowledge based world.

Such a change carries implications for the structure of work within the overall economy of a nation. Figure 1 shows the transition from a largely agricultural economy to a post-industrial economy and its implications for the structure of the workforce. It is a conceptual map, not a statistical map – the size of each of the 'boxes' is meant to represent the shape and structure of the workforce and their influence over the economic life of a nation (the lower down the list, the lower the influence).

We are currently in the final stages of the penultimate column – the information age. Yet our education system was designed for the industrial age. We are now seeking to transform it and change it so that it meets the needs of the information age. Yet the information age is ending and we are quietly (but quickly) moving into the age of robotics and biotechnology. The structure of work and the nature of society will be very different some fifty years from now, when the coming age is truly showing its 'colours'.

Some of the categories of activity within the various economic frameworks shown below may be alien to some readers – "cultural sycophants", for example (meaning those who talk and write about culture but are not creative artists – food critics being a good example) or bio-med workers (those who work in bio factories producing medical solutions, such as stem-cell grown body organs, for example). But rather than focus on detail, it makes more sense to look at the big picture. Our economy is more complex with more roles and functions requiring knowledge and skill than was the case in the industrial age. That is the message.

complexity theory

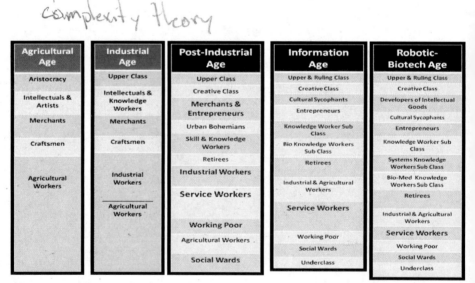

Agricultural Age	Industrial Age	Post-Industrial Age	Information Age	Robotic-Biotech Age
Aristocracy	Upper Class	Upper Class	Upper & Ruling Class	Upper & Ruling Class
Intellectuals & Artists	Intellectuals & Knowledge Workers	Creative Class	Creative Class	Creative Class
Merchants	Merchants	Merchants & Entrepreneurs	Cultural Sycophants	Developers of Intellectual Goods
Craftsmen	Craftsmen	Urban Bohemians	Entrepreneurs	Cultural Sycophants
Agricultural Workers	Industrial Workers	Skill & Knowledge Workers	Knowledge Worker Sub Class	Entrepreneurs
	Agricultural Workers	Retirees	Bio Knowledge Workers Sub Class	Knowledge Worker Sub Class
		Industrial Workers	Retirees	Systems Knowledge Workers Sub Class
		Service Workers	Industrial & Agricultural Workers	Bio-Med Knowledge Workers Sub Class
		Working Poor	Service Workers	Retirees
		Agricultural Workers	Working Poor	Industrial & Agricultural Workers
		Social Wards	Social Wards	Service Workers
			Underclass	Working Poor
				Social Wards
				Underclass

Figure 1: The Structure of Work and Power in Different Eras of the Economy

There is a growing view that the human capital requirements of the twenty first century global knowledge economy (so called 'twenty first century skills') are different from the human capital needs of the previous century. These differences are usually presented in terms of citizens being both consumers and producers (so called "*prosumers*"), and of global connectivity; social networking, team skills and critical thinking are said to be sufficiently distinctive to require curriculum reform[16]. Others have suggested these twenty first century skills are not so much new skills as they are different descriptors of excellent teaching practices as seen in the work many schools have been pursuing since Montessori, particularly those involving critical thinking creativity and problem solving. Nonetheless, the twenty first century skills are seen to be a human capital strategy requiring a different approach to the content and process of learning.

The critical voices suggest that a focus on process skills rather than core competencies implied by the twenty first century skills movement is seriously flawed. They offer four basic criticisms: (a) that there is a forced separation between knowledge and skills; (b) that teachers are capable of working on complex problems beyond their cognitive abilities but are not empowered to do so ; (c) that experience is erroneously treated as equivalent to practice; and (d) that communities and organizations in the twenty first century need knowledge and skills that are very similar, if not the same, as those they have needed for the last twenty five years (Willingham, 2009). Despite these clear concerns, many jurisdictions are making significant changes to the curriculum requirements for schools and are investing in the professional development of teachers to better equip them for twenty first century learning and teaching activities.

Cases for experiential education

As the global economy is in the midst of a great reset, there are significant related changes that are reshaping how the world works. In addition to major demographic challenges, we are seeing changes in the balance of power, changes in the stability of regions (especially the Middle East, but also parts of Asia), the emergence of new super-economic powers (Brazil, Russia, India and China – the so called BRICS economies) as well as a decline in the functionality of global institutions, such as the UN, IMF and the World Bank. While some see these developments as catastrophic, others (myself included[17]) see them as evidence of a renaissance age; an age in transition. Indeed, Murgatroyd and Simpson have written about this extensively and see signs that amidst major structural change in the world economy, there are signs of renaissance everywhere[18].

Technology

The third driver of the sense that change is needed in our education system is technology. The Apple *iPad* is the fastest selling technology ever made. One million *iPad1* devices were sold in twenty eight days (April 2010) and its successor, the *iPad2*, reached this target in three days (March 2011). 19.5 million were sold in one year. There are over 400,000 applications available for the *iPad* and *iPhone* and the one billionth download of an application occurred in January 2011. One piece of social media software – *Facebook* – has attracted over 640 million users.

These data suggest the scale of information technology penetration. But this is not the only way in which technology is changing the way we work and play...In health care, robots are being used to support (and in some cases, conduct) surgical procedures. In North America, some 75,000 robotic procedures are conducted each year. Every car sold in Europe and North America is now enabled by digital technology – gears, electrical systems, entertainment systems and other on-board devices are managed by computers. The Airbus fleet of aeroplanes are powered by what is known as "fly-by-wire"; computer assisted and machine intelligence driven devices that control the systems from take off to landing, with the opportunity for human over-rides. Our entertainment – whether television, radio, film or music – makes extensive use of technology. Whether it is the special effects on films like *Harry Potter*, the digital recordings of Mahler's song cycle, internet radio, CNN news – technology is ubiquitous. It is also changing how many industries work. Take the video / DVD industry: major high street video and DVD rental agencies like *Blockbuster* have been replaced by internet based providers like *iTunes* and *Netflix*.

Our young people are heavily engaged with technology. Reports suggest that young people spend between 20 and 40 hours engaged with digital media (including television) each week[19]; more time than they spend at school during formal school time. Indeed, colleagues at the University of Delft in the Netherlands have suggested, based on neuropsychological studies, that young people are beginning to be "wired" differently; their brain functions in different ways as a result of their exposure to digital media and devices. The Delft team refer to this in terms of a species difference – homo-*zappiens* rather than homo-sapiens[20].

There are other drivers; the rising costs of public education; the perception that the growing complexity of knowledge requires a rethink of curriculum; the quality of teacher education and teaching; the increasing urbanization of society and its impact on small rural schools; the costs of technology; demographics;

economic austerity; inequities between rich and poor; aboriginal and non aboriginal; women and men – are all factors in the clamour for change. But these three are the most substantial drivers for educational change and reform. Let us explore these themes a little more.

Alberta is not an untypical school jurisdiction. It has some 600,000 students and spends app. $6.3 billion (€4 billion) on compulsory schooling. Over the last decade it has spent some $1.87 billion (€1.2 billion) on technology for schools, including investments in network infrastructure, a learning objects repository, video conference networks and lap top programs. While some of these investments have been directly connected to specific change agendas (the Alberta Initiatives' for School Improvement (AISI), for example[21]) others have been generalized investments responding to a perceived need to make technology available. The impact of such investments appears marginal and they have certainly not led to any major change in how schools as organizations across the jurisdiction function.

But technology is changing quickly. The development of the semantic web, hand held and mobile devices increasingly used for learning and education and the emergence of robotics for learning and teaching are all seen to create opportunities to change the processes by which learning takes place and knowledge is used in the process of discovery, innovation and the development of understanding. Jurisdictions are struggling to find the balance between teachers, technology and process for effective learning.

Our Students are Changing

agreed

Another factor leading us to seek change in our school system is the changing nature of the student body; the human capital that is an 'input' to the school system. Students beginning school in September 2011 will retire from the workforce between 2071 and 2081, if they enter it at all. Unlike their great grandfathers, most will occupy some 15-20 jobs in their work-life and stay no more than five to seven years with a single employer. Work-life balance for many of this *iGen* (also known as the *"text generation"* or *Generation Z*) will be a bigger issue than pensions. They will expect their employer to practice strategically focused human resource policies which aid their personal and professional development and will look to work as one source of satisfaction, but work will not be the focus for their life. They will bring to their work remarkable technical skills, a strong entrepreneurial outlook, a deep-seated social consciousness (especially with respect to the environment), and, like every 'new' generation, a healthy dose of questioning and a desire for change.

This generation will understand the power of social networks, cloud based computing and technology and will have a high level of absorption for such technologies in terms of facilitating work and social transactions, changing work practices and engaging in global conversations (Palfrey, 2008; Tapscott, 2008). They will have these skills despite their school systems, which in general currently appear largely unable to engage these technologies in powerful ways in the pursuit of learning, knowledge and understanding. Indeed, many school systems are outlawing social networking technologies, seeing them (sometimes with good reason) as distractions. The *iGen* will also be quick to leverage the fast emergence of machine and artificial intelligence as well as domestic and social robotics – they will 'get' change as a constant in a way that the current generation of leaders and managers still find difficult; and in so doing, challenge current managerial assumptions about the nature and function of human capital.

A particular strength of the iGen will be their ability to multitask, to network globally and to assimilate complex information and ideas from a range of different sources. As the world becomes increasing globalized[22], this generation will progressively engage what is known as the "neurosphere" [23]or "singularity"[24]– the integration of intelligent machines with human intelligence. Yet their schooling will not have well prepared them for the challenge of such integration, unless things change. As Sir Kenneth Robinson observes [25], schools are in fact preparing young people for jobs that do not yet exist which will require skills we don't fully understand and use technologies which are in the process of being invented, yet these same schools behave as if the economic need for human capital has not changed since the turn of the twentieth century.

The iGen will also be familiar with some of the basic concepts of design. Many of them will own their own web space, will be familiar with social networks and will have created a weblog (blog), which they will have customized or directly designed. They will also be increasingly aware of design as a question of choices and deliberate decisions – especially as these decisions relate to the environment, technology, living spaces and clothing. They will have personalized their hand held digital device through a unique combination of applications, self design covers and add-on features. One teacher suggested that "this is not simply a different generation, it is a different species", which has led some researchers to term the iGen "homo-zappiens" [26], reflecting not just different learning styles but also a distinctive psychobiology. These homo-zappiens will provide the basis for human capital development in our communities and economies – they are already, through their behavior, changing the way some industries work[27].

An In Between Time (eco tone / edge)

We need to understand the systems dynamics of what is happening in developed world education systems. We can so by understanding such systems in terms of the 'S' curve.

The 'S' curve is a systems model used to describe the stages of development of maturing systems. It uses two dimensions – time (the horizontal dimension) and outcomes (the vertical dimension) and plots progress of a system over time. The basic model is shown below as Figure 2. Stages of development are shown as numbers on this simple diagram and many commentators would suggest that we are at stage 4 of this model.

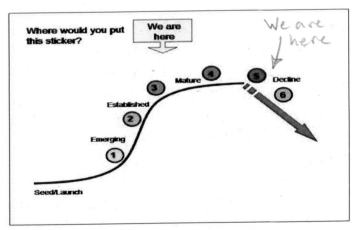

Figure Two: The S Curve Framework for Understanding the Maturation of Systems

Typically, there are two 'solutions' to being at this point in the development of a maturing system. The first and most common is to seek performance and productivity gains within the framework of the system "as is": tweaking the system so as to sustain it. There are many examples of this in education; adding capacities to support the school such as teacher assistants; teaching aids for special needs children; enhanced technology; new curriculum; performance-based pay for teachers; and so on.

The alternative is to seek to develop a new and alternative system which the system can switch to at some tipping point. We show what this looks like in Figure 3 below. Again there are several examples of this in educational reform – the privatization of schools in Sweden, the development of Charter Schools throughout North America, the development of Academies in England and so on. Each of these developments are alternative systems of educational provision which, it is proposed, the 'old' system could switch to once the 'new' system is a proven success.

The difficulty is that it has taken over one hundred years to establish the current system. In Britain, for example, the basis of the core public educational system was established through the 1944 Education Act, building on previous legislation and modified by the comprehensive schools movement of the 1960's – and it takes time for 'alternative' systems to become mainstream.

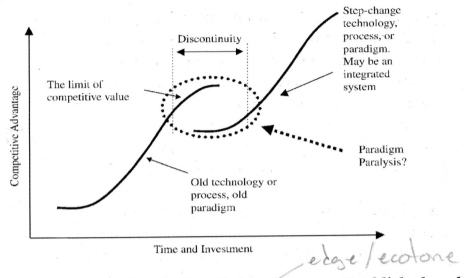

Figure Three: The Tipping Points Between Established and Emerging Systems

The gap between the period of decline of the established system and the emergence of an alternative is known in systems thinking as the "in between time" – a messy and difficult time when systems compete, resources are competitively sought and performance in either system is not optimal.

There is also the issue of risk. While some will have confidence in the new system, the experience of the majority of those who have the challenge of administering and operating the system is in the old system, at least for a considerable time. They have to unlearn the rules of engagement and develop new approaches and understandings so as to maximize the outcomes of the new system. While many may commit to doing so, it is actually hard to do so.

For example, in the current old system of education in some countries there are public assessments of performance at key stages – for examples in Grades 3, 6, 9 and 12 in some Canadian jurisdictions. In the new system, such testing of all students at these key stages may be seen as inappropriate, but the demands from the public and their representatives to continue with these tests will be considerable: after all, "it was good enough before".

Another example is that of gateways. In almost all mature education systems there is a split at various points; elementary school; junior high; high school; college or university; work based training; employment. In a new system, such distinctions may be passé. Students may progress according to ability and achievements, passing through apprenticeship, for example, while still at high school or working full time while at receiving a college education. As the gateways blur, so do issues about funding and curriculum. Managers who were skilled at making the old system work, find the new system difficult and outcomes often decline in the first phase of the introduction of new systems for this reason.

The Transformative Journey

Some educational leaders, in their response to this "in between time", speak of the need to transform education – it is a frequent theme of the State of the Union address by Presidents of the United States since Roosevelt. Marc Tucker of the National Centre on Education and the Economy makes an interesting observation about this rhetoric. Noting the reforms which are currently underway during the Presidency of Barrack Obama in the United States, he says:

> "there is no evidence that any country that leads the world's educational performance league tables has gotten there by implementing any of the major agenda items that

dominate the educational reform agenda in the United States"[28]

Many of the transformative steps; vouchers; Charter Schools; educational entrepreneurs to be systems disrupters; outcome based funding; value added assessment; performance-based pay; a focus on 21st century skills; reform of professional development and teacher education; personalized learning systems; online learning...we could go on – are imposed as "reforms" that *may* work rather than reforms which are emerging from evidence based experiments which are rigorous and systematic. If these reforms were new pharmaceutical prescriptions, they would never secure the regulatory approvals required for a new drug. Yet we impose such reforms in the hope that they will be transformative without reference to their side effects.

Doing so speaks to a lack of understanding of the transformative journey. Such journeys have a number of stages, each of which are complex and difficult to manage. Typically, such journeys involve these steps:

expanding the community edge.

1. **Identifying and 'Selling' the Challenge** – There is a need for stakeholders and those directly engaged in a current "old" system to identify and understand why the system needs to change. If these elements are assumed, then resistance will be high and challenges long-lasting. Selling the problem without pushing a solution is a necessary first step to sustainable reform. **Building Ownership of the Challenge and the Need to Change** – Knowing there is a problem is one thing. Engaging people in the work of finding solutions is another. Citizen engagement (not just

of those who currently control public education) is a second step to transformation.

2. **Systematically Exploring Options for Solution** – Rather than 'sales pitching an idea', there is a need for rigorous evidence based scanning of what is working and what alternatives are available to the current system. For example, exploring why Finland has consistently been amongst the highest performing educational jurisdictions in the world and seeking to understand the lessons of that model is a helpful task[29] – not that one can 'rent' a system change from another place, but one *can* learn from their journey. Such evidence based exploration can be used to build ownership and consensus. While many will disagree with many of the options explored, placing evidence of what works elsewhere in the world in front of them is a powerful way of engaging in an evidence based conversation aimed at building momentum around the need for change. At this stage, some of the change options are often 'taken off the table', since they garner no support.

3. **Using Evidence to Determine a Course of Action** – The evidence based conversation and engagement of stakeholders at step 3 above permits specific courses of action to be identified. Once the key strategies have been identified, a systematic approach to roll-out of these plans is needed.

4. **Piloting Action to Determine Success** –Systems cannot be changed overnight, despite the desire of many to do so. What is proven to work are pilot projects with early adopters who secure demonstrable success and become beacons for the next group of adopters. We know a great deal about adoption of new ways of working. It looks like

the graph shown in Figure 4 below. The vertical axis is the adoption of a new system, process, or technology and the horizontal axis is time.

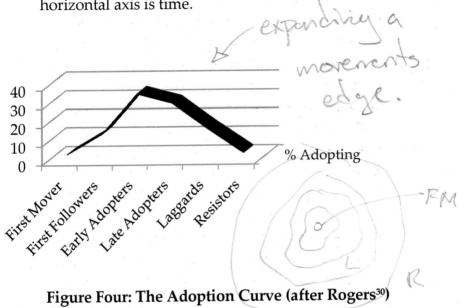

expanding a movements edge.

Figure Four: The Adoption Curve (after Rogers[30])

What this figure suggests is that it takes a considerable time to engage 84% of those involved in a system in a new way of doing things and that you require the pull of the first 16% to enable the others to join. Whatever the change, it is rarely possible to secure upwards of 84% in short order. Piloting to show promise and performance is a key to effective *sustainable* transformation. In Ontario in the late 1960s and early 1970s, the pilot of a new approach to high school took the form of some significant high schools being challenged to secure specific learning outcomes while being exempt from normal regulatory and system controls (except for those relating to health and safety and those regulated by teacher contracts). The result was a variety of significant changes which produced substantially higher levels of educational attainment than was the case for the regulated schools. Once the specific ingredients of success were identified, the regulatory regimes were modified to permit all schools to replicate these successes.

5. **Tweaking to Secure Maximum Impact** – Not all pilots will be perfect. There is a need to tweak and adjust the work of the pilot activity so that it overcomes known problems and minimizes identified risks. Once tweaked however, system wide reform begins to be possible.

6. **Rolling Out on a Large Scale** – Once pilot projects have demonstrated their merit and the model has been tweaked, it is ready for large scale roll-out. Not all will be 'ready', so system wide roll out will often be phased by region or other category (elementary, junior high, etc). The aim, however, is to secure system wide change within a certain period of time.

Most educational reformers are frustrated by this journey – they want action and they want it now. Just read the text of speeches by Ministers of Education or the Secretary of Education in the United States. They use language of urgency and commitment to seek to accelerate the journey. But on system wide large scale reform, the journey requires time: there are no quick fixes.

Indeed, many fixes offered as "rapid improvements" have a track record of significant failure.

The Dog who Does not Bark

Conan Doyle, author of Sherlock Homes, wrote a story called the *Sliver Blade* in which the silent dog is the clue to unravelling the mystery. . In educational change and transformation the role of the silent dog is generally played by the students. Students are often seen as the "victims" of reform movements or as the intended beneficiaries; rarely as the drivers of reform or as part of the team engineering the changes which will have a radical impact on them and their successors as students.

Yet their knowledge of the system and its weaknesses is considerable and their expertise (especially in terms of leveraging technology, for example) often surpasses that of many of the adults who are engaged in change. If we are to secure sustainable transformation of education so as to do better, prepare our young people for citizenship in a global knowledge economy and leverage technology to support their learning and development, then they need to be engaged in every stage of the transformation journey. If they are not, we are already missing a key feature of the global knowledge economy: change and innovation comes from everywhere and most often from creative, young people.

Larry Page and Sergey Brin were 25 years old when they founded *Google Inc.* Mark Zuckerberg was 20 years old when he co-founded *Facebook.* The three co-founders of *YouTube*, all former *PayPal* employees, were in the mid to late twenties when they founded the most viewed video site on the World Wide Web. All were entrepreneurs, all were young, and all used a combination of knowledge, skill and understanding to create products and services which have changed the way we experience the World Wide Web. None were part of the *establishment*.

Andrew Mason is the founder of *Groupon* as well as *The Point*, the collective action platform from which *Groupon* was born. *Groupon* is the fastest growing technology company ever to have been created and currently has 7,000 employees worldwide. Andrew's mostly unremarkable existence began in Pittsburgh, PA. He moved to Chicago in 1999 to attend Northwestern University, where he lives today. Andrew graduated with a degree in music and became a software developer through no ambition of his own, but via a series of acquaintances offering to give him money to do incrementally harder stuff on computers. Excited by the power of technology to change the world, Andrew developed *Policy Tree*, a policy debate visualization tool, and won a scholarship to attend the University of Chicago and the Harris School of Public Policy in 2006. In school for only 3 months, Andrew dropped out after receiving an unexpected offer to fund the idea that would become *The Point*. The Point, a ground-breaking approach to online collective action and fundraising, launched in November 2007. One year later, Andrew founded *Groupon*, leveraging the collective buying technology of *The Point* to make it easier (and cheaper) to experience all the great stuff in Chicago and, more recently, the rest of the world. *Groupon* as a company is now estimated to be worth $25 billion; grown from nothing in 2008.

Most disruptive innovation does not come from those with designated roles such as executives in firms, universities or colleges, or from research and development teams, or from system leaders. Disruptive innovation comes from either those nearest the 'customer'; or from 'customers' themselves – those

The edge contains the most potential for growth.

who understand latent needs and opportunities, who can see a way of delivering products or services in a way that is efficient, effective and profitable; or it comes from outsiders who look at a known problem and see a new way of solving it. If transformation is intended to be transformative, it is likely to be disruptive. There is a need to involve those who understand the system best in the work of change.

This transformative journey in education and the fact that the world in general (but educational systems in particular), is experiencing this "in between time" are the starting points for a new renaissance in education. In the 'messy firmament of change and transformation, there are beacons and exemplars of outstanding success that we need to find and understand so that the renaissance can be sustained. Whether it is small examples: an elementary school that is built in the same facility as a seniors home, where the seniors listen to every child read every day and where each child is not only a year ahead of their physical year in reading ability but 75% of the seniors have stopped heart disease related medications since they no longer have high blood pressure or high cholesterol levels – or large examples of major systems changes which work, we can see evidence of the renaissance everywhere. The challenge is to sustain it.

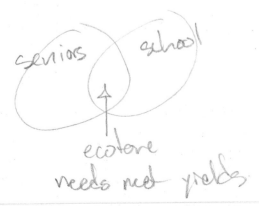

The Challenge

The challenge, then, is to engage in a systematic journey for educational change and development which reflects a response to the three big challenges - do better; prepare our young people for citizenship and work in the global knowledge economy; and leverage technology in doing so – through the development of a sustainable, effective and quality educational process accessible to all. This is not an easy challenge.

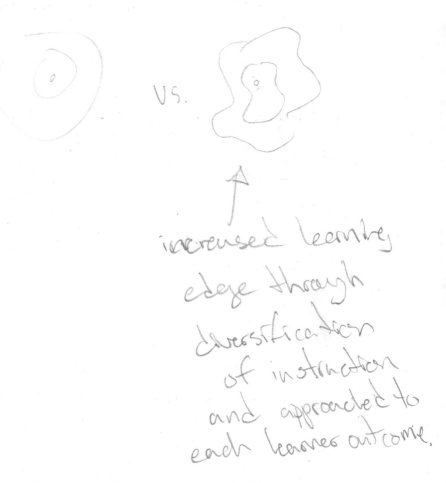

VS.

increased learning edge through diversification of instruction and approaches to each learner outcome.

Chapter 2

What is a School For?

This may sound like a strange question to some ("it's where students go to learn, right?") but it is actually a complex question. In this chapter we will explore a range of functions performed by and within a school and look critically at the future of the school as a social learning centred institution. The aim of this chapter is to set the stage for the key arguments for educational reform.

A key proposition of this chapter is that, while teachers have many admirable qualities, they are not superhuman. Our expectations of teachers go far beyond what any reasonable citizen should realistically expect teachers and educators to achieve. It is not surprising, then, that fewer teachers are staying in the profession for a life-time and that many teachers report considerable stress. One recent study shows that, a typical teacher in school jurisdiction will spend fifty five hours a week working, twenty one (38%) of which involve working with students [31]. Teacher stress and burn-out affect 41% of the profession[32].

The School as a Central Hub in a Community

In rural communities, schools are not just where children go to receive their required education. They are the true social hubs of communities.

creating resilient teachers.

When this author moved from a large urban city in South Wales (Cardiff – population 341,064) to a small rural community in Northern Alberta (Town of Athabasca – population 2,575), our children's school and the activities it supported was our 'way in' to the community. This is how we met other parents, how our children bonded with life-long friends and where two young boys from Wales learned about their new country – Canada – and the special place within Canada known as Alberta. It is where the values of the community were not simply taught, but experienced every day.

When we later moved to a large urban City in Alberta (Edmonton – population 900,000+) so that our children could attend the high school of their choice, the position of the school in the community was not as central, but still important. Victoria School for the Arts ("Vic" to its alumni, staff and students) was and is a legendary place specializing in the creative arts and encouraging a range of arts careers; film production; music; dance; art; sculpture; electronic arts; game development; and virtual reality – as adjuncts and vehicles for the provincial curriculum. It also has a strong sports reputation, hosting a major international basketball tournament each year. For young artistically inclined teenagers, Vic was the place to go. Social networks were built and maintained (even before Facebook and MySpace and You Tube), connections to the arts community were enabled, and even alumni came back to give encouragement, which is how we met the actor Leslie Nielson.

In Athabasca, the elementary and high schools were hubs for the community as a whole; in Edmonton Vic was a hub for young people interested in the arts in the broadest sense. In both, social

schools are places for increasing connections.

networks were developed and sustained and life-long friendships were established.

When a school closes, something of the community dies with it. Small rural communities, often experiencing depopulation and the departure of its most talented youth, find it difficult to sustain a school for students of all ages. Students are often bussed great distances once they complete elementary education, especially if they have special needs. Though the bus itself is part of the school experience, as any student will tell you, travelling two hours each way to school somewhat changes that experience.

The School and Values Transmission

At the heart of the idea of the school as a hub in the community is the idea that the school is a place which sustains the values of that community. Schools are themselves symbols of these values. For example, despite being a small community, the County of Athabasca (total population around 10,000 including the Town) had a vibrant Francophone community. They wanted this reflected in the way in which the school operated and, for a certain period of time, the school offered a French immersion program to support this community, thus reflecting the bilingual nature of Canada and the desire within the community as a whole to support the Francophone's.

In other communities, other values are strongly reflected. These may be spiritual values, values associated with healthy living, values associated with care and concern for self and others (sometimes cloaked in the term "emotional intelligence") or the values of social inclusion. What students learn about themselves and the values of their communities is often implicit in the way the school functions and the way in which adults and students interact and through peer interaction. Occasionally, values will also be the subject of teaching and learning activities. But the first and major function of a school is to be a hub of the community for the transmission of values.

The School and Social Support

A student colleague, now Emeritus Professor Jim Mansell of the Tizard Centre at the University of Kent, was a pioneer of the inclusion into ordinary classrooms and the community of those with special needs, including challenging psychological conditions. He has written about this work extensively[33] and was the principal author of the *Mansell Report* (1992, revised 2007) for the UK Department of Health. His life's work has been to see those with disabilities integrated into society at every level.

As a result of this movement, which began in the early 1960s and gathered momentum over the next two decades before becoming widely accepted, schools are a place where the abilities and disabilities of young people are fully assessed. In Canada, for example, children with special needs are "coded" so that their needs can be served by the allocation of appropriate resources – different codes attract different levels of resources. These assessments, which cover psycho-social disabilities as well as physical disabilities, are thorough and complex but should result in needed resources being made available to support student integration into the classroom[34].

each student has a need + yields.

But it is not just such disabilities as dyslexia, autism or cerebral palsy that are assessed in this way. The social conditions of learners – their social needs – are also assessed. A surprisingly large number of young persons arrive at school without breakfast or without the means to secure a lunch. School food programs have been established in many places as part of the school day. Now other social and health needs are being met through the school system and its partnership with social workers, dental hygienists, medical professionals, and rehabilitation therapists.

One strong example of this service function is the work many schools are undertaking to combat childhood obesity and its correlates; early onset diabetes and heart disease. Some schools are using their educational and health resources, together with social programs, to provide a basis for students to understand the fact that "you are what you eat" and, while some genetic factors are at play, diet and exercise remain key to physical health.

Schools provide needs to students.

The School and 'Self'

A key function of schooling as a process and experience is to provide a significant aid to individual students in understanding who they are and what they want to become. While not all come away with this understanding, it has been a feature of educational philosophy that the process of learning and schooling is also one of self-discovery.

To some extent, schools have been diverted from this work by a focus on 'self-esteem', wrongly interpreting the child as a fragile 'self' which needs constant nurturing and protection from bruising, damage or pain.

providing options/

connections

Our job is to increase this resiliency

Humans have a great capacity for resilience. They can withstand a great deal of challenge, threat and uncertainty and they do so because they experience these things throughout their lives, especially in childhood. By seeking to protect children – not offend them, fail them, challenge them, put them in pass/fail or win/loose situations, support them in as many ways as possible – we may be slowing the growth of their resilience and effective coping skills. The psychologist, Lori Gottlieb, writing in *The Atlantic*, captures this challenge in her article *How to Land Your Kid in Therapy*[35]. Speaking of the consequences of parents and teachers who spend their time nurturing and caring for their kids' self-esteem and writing as a psychologist, she says:

> "We were running ourselves ragged in a herculean effort to do right by our kids—yet what seemed like grown-up versions of them were sitting in our offices, saying they felt empty, confused, and anxious. Back in graduate school, the clinical focus had always been on how the *lack* of parental attunement affects the child. It never occurred to any of us to ask, what if the parents are *too* attuned? What happens to *those* kids?"

Others speak of parents who helicopter over their children so as to protect them from threat, challenge or disruptions. The result, according to Gottlieb and others[36], is a growing number of 20's and 30's individuals who are suffering from depression and anxiety, have difficulty choosing or committing to a satisfying career path, struggle with relationships, and just generally feel a sense of emptiness or lack of purpose.

To develop resilience, young people need to experience success and failure, to be unsuccessful at some things and successful at others, to be told facts about themselves which they may not find easy to hear, to see themselves as others really see them; not some version of themselves which they know in their inner-life to be untrue. Harry Gray, another psychologist and founder of *The Grove*, once suggested that "all significant learning about ourselves comes from pain and failure", explaining that this is how we find our boundaries, often surprising ourselves in the process. Some learning about our self can also come from what he called "earned success", where a process of success mixed with failure, false starts, and trials of will leads to a successful outcome. In short, we learn through genuine and often challenging experiences.

Schools help with the process of becoming a self aware person in several ways.

First, they provide a setting in which an individual can compare and contrast their own thoughts, feelings and experiences with others of the same age.

Second, in interactions with adults, individual learners can develop and test their 'self' in language, behaviour and peer interactions.

Third, by exploring ideas and developing skills, learners can test themselves against their own assumptions about what they can and can't do ("I think I will be great at playing the piano" only to find six months later that it is quite the instrument to master), which is why honest and direct feedback is important.

Fourth, by providing curriculum choices, young people can test in a safe environment their understanding of certain futures; career aspirations, for example.

Fifth, through project work, sports and extra curricular activities, young people begin to understand the roles they can and cannot play on teams; they understand their behavioural styles and the limitations their style creates on their social interactions.

Finally, through formal and informal assessment, provided they are realistic and not "adjusted for self-esteem" reasons, young people are 'reality tested' each time they sit a test, examination or compete in a challenging activity.

This is a major and critical function of schooling. Much of the character of a young person is set during kindergarten and elementary school. The remaining years of schooling confirm or challenge the 'self' created in these early years. It is a function which needs to be taken as seriously as learning a subject.

School as a Pathfinder

A specific sub-set of the developing understanding of 'self', as outlined above, is the beginning of the development of a pathway to adulthood and career. School is seen by many as a transitional hub; the gateway to the next stage of career development.

This is not to say that school has to be focused on career, work related skills and employability. Only that this is seen by many to be a part of the function of the school. In fact, many young people leave school at the end of compulsory schooling and do not seriously pursue college or university level learning afterwards. In Canada, for instance, the dropout rate from first year college or university averages around 15% and completion rates for apprenticeships are low[37]. For many young people, K-12 *is* their education.

A small number of students know their career goals for sure early in life and relentlessly pursue them. Others flounder in the face of the world of work. We know that the patterns of employment have changed significantly: a young person entering the workforce today is likely to hold twenty five to thirty different positions in their career and is also likely to have periods of unemployment. At the time of writing this chapter, for example, 38.5 million Canadian, EU and US citizens are out of work[38]. We also know that life-time employment with the same employer is largely a thing of the past.

The key task for the school is to build the skills required to make work related choices and to establish and develop resilience and coping skills with respect to work. "Careers guidance" has been replaced by job skills in many school programs.

School as a Learning to Learn Centre

One thing schools do is to establish a process for learning. This usually involves the implicit development of learning skills, since learning to learn is not, unfortunately, a subject which schools spend much time on. Though things have improved since the days when left handed children were forced to write with their right hand (a practice which continued in Britain until the mid 1950's), different learning styles are not well accommodated in school systems.

The primary method of learning to learn is by meeting the expectations set by teachers. Most teachers use a variety of methods in their classrooms to secure learning outcomes. These range from personal project work (the book review, the essay, the montage, the science experiment), team work, reading assignments and so on. Textbooks and Wikipedia are seen by learners as core sources of knowledge, with teachers regarded as "bringing to life" the meaning of ideas and supporting the learners' development of understanding. Testing and assessments are seen as arbitrating learning; assessing mastery, not necessary competence or sustainable skill development.

Many schools have chosen to pursue problem-based learning and problem-focused learning as a basis for a great deal of their learning activity, especially at the elementary and junior high levels. They understand the power of real life problems as tools for carrying a range of curriculum and teaching options – the more 'wicked' the problem focused on, the more the learning that is possible[39]. Examples include a focus on reducing water consumption by 25% in a community, developing a strategy for ending loneliness amongst seniors in a region, a project to install solar power for the school linked to a demonstration of cost-savings and life-cycle CO_2 reductions – each of these examples are illustrative of the way in which a design focused process, which uses critical thinking, innovation and creativity as the core methodologies for inquiry based learning, focus on meaningful community challenges and engage young people as part of the solution to these challenges. Each of these requires student engagement, authenticity, rigour (as evidenced by both formative and summative assessment), engagement beyond the school, active exploration using appropriate technologies, a strong and meaningful connection to others (especially adults) with appropriate expertise, teamwork and elaborated communication as well as an element of fun and a lot of imagination.

But not all learning is like this. For many, especially learners who feel a need to move while learning (we call these learners dancers; ballet schools are full of them), or to learn by creating (artists) or by doing (artisans), schools are textbook based and rigid places. They do not meet their learning to learn needs at all. Our literature and culture is full of these stories: the novel *A Kestrel for a Knave* [40] (which became Ken Loach's film *Kes*) describes how a young boy found meaning in his work with a Kestrel and this was more important to him than schooling; the play and film *Billy Elliot* [41] describe a northern British boy's preoccupation with dance and movement and how this was a compelling force in his life. There are more novels, films and stories which reflect the lack of connection between the person and their school. *lack of connection in the current model*

Not everyone can learn in a class setting. Groups are difficult places for those learners who prefer self-managed learning or to learn at their own pace. Group discussion can also be difficult for learners who are shy, find speaking in public difficult (when asked, adults say that their biggest fear is having to speak in public) or who need to think through their ideas before making them public.

While schools are increasingly embracing a limited use of technology – *SmartBoards*® are in many classrooms and there are several one lap top per child projects running, with some schools now offering *iPads* to every student – what has not occurred on a widespread basis is a transformation of learning as a process from "batch processing" (classes of 20-40 students, year based groupings or grades, common graduation dates) to personalized or individualized learning. Nor are many schools permitting students to engage in their own learning activities through work (many school students work part-time) or their own activities and recognizing this learning for credit, though there is a growing movement aimed at enabling this to occur.

Learning to learn is *not* currently a preoccupation of schools, but it is their implicit work.

School as a Centre for Creativity and Imagination

Walk into any elementary school and you will generally see art work on the walls in every classroom. Drawing, paintings, and sculptures will also be displayed. We may also hear music, singing and see dancing.

Walk into most high schools or secondary schools and you may see some art, may attend a music class and, on special occasions, be shown the art and sculpture done by students. You will rarely see dance.

Somewhere between kindergarten and grade 12 the spirit of creativity and a passion for fine arts gets side-tracked into 'optional' activity. Why?

The most common explanation is that the curriculum demands of high school, most especially for those intending to go on to college or university, are so demanding that "we do not have time" for all of the subjects we would like to teach. Art and music are usually the first casualties in this war for money, time and talent. The second explanation that is generally offered is that, by around age fourteen, students preferences are for more academic or technical (trades) subjects than for creative arts, so student choice dictates the position of these creative subjects in the league table of resourcing.

Creative students create their own links

What is not said is that employers are increasingly looking for evidence that the people they hire have creative abilities and can work in teams, and that the creative spirit is as important in many positions (especially if the employee moves into management positions) as technical skill. While creativity can take many forms, nurturing the creative spirit is, to employers, a key role for schools.

Sir Ken Robinson's talk at TED[42] is one of the most viewed TED talks since that innovative program began, and his Royal Society of Arts and Manufacturing animation[43] has also been widely viewed. In these presentations, he argues that art and music are as important as maths and science in the educational priorities of a nation. More specifically, he positions creativity and imagination as central requirements for citizenship in the twenty first century. According to Robinson, school's first duty is to enable young people to explore their talents to the full in the safe environment of the school.

Some school systems, such as that in Oklahoma, understand this and are seeking to find creativity across the curriculum and opportunities for integrating creativity and the arts in the way they offer their programs. The Minister of Education for Singapore, in a private conversation, made clear that the next

Creative learners build their own links and thus their own resiliency

stage of the development of curriculum in that country – a top performing jurisdiction on the PISA analysis – needs to find new opportunities to develop the creative spirit.

Nurturing the creative spirit is a key role for schools across the curriculum.

School as Knowledge Centres

Schools engage teachers to teach. They teach a curriculum, set in many countries by the accountable government agency. The national curriculum (or the state or provincial curriculum) sets out what it is learners should learn when as well as how that learning should be assessed.

The extent to which the curriculum is specified varies considerably by jurisdiction. In Finland, for example, the Department of Education set out the broad framework of the curriculum, leaving the work of determining just what to teach when and how to their teachers. Shanghai, Japan and Singapore have recently made significant revisions to their required curriculum regimes so that students at each stage of learning balance a high level of content mastery with problem-solving, an ability to demonstrate independent thought, creativity and innovation. Indeed, the assessment regimes in these nations test all of these facets of learning[44].

In the US there is no national curriculum and many States have left curriculum matters to individual school boards, though the federal government is now requiring states using federal funds to test at grade levels in mathematics and English (the Common Core Standards), with important consequences tied to student performance. The focus of these tests, unlike those in Shanghai, Singapore, Japan and Finland, is on knowledge mastery rather than the more advanced imagineering skills. The US also seeks to use computer scored assessments for curriculum, while most other nations either do not or are limiting the use of these tests. Rather they focus on trigger questions and ask students to respond in writing with statements or short essays or problem solutions which show their thinking processes.

What is clear, when these curriculum systems are reviewed, is the following:

1. Traditional subjects – mother tongue, social studies, mathematics, science and language arts – taught as academic subjects remain dominant.
2. There is an emerging trend to integrate technological skills across the curriculum, though some systems see this as a subject in its own right.
3. A substantial push for the curriculum in those jurisdictions which have a national / state curriculum comes from the entry requirements of universities and colleges, especially with respect to the teaching of mathematics and science.
4. Some subjects which one might think every school learner should know; financial literacy; social skills; emotional intelligence; critical thinking; design; healthy eating; nutrition and cooking; child rearing – are not taught to all (if at all).
5. Skills required for trades are seen as a "second tier" choice in terms of resource allocation and funding, even though the demand for qualified trades persons is growing faster than the demand for many professions. The emphasis of

most systems remains on post-secondary gateways to college and university.

6. Textbooks – whether e-books or printed texts – remain the primary vehicle through which teachers secure a knowledge base for learning and textbook publishers remain a powerful influence over what gets taught.

7. What gets assessed gets taught. In those systems which make use of high stakes or standardized testing, what teachers think will be tested gets a lot more attention than those things which may not be tested but which students find interesting. Indeed, "teaching to the test" is seen as a major problem in systems which test frequently (i.e. in grades 3,6,9 and 12).

8. Not all who teach a subject may be qualified to do so in terms of their own higher education, especially in the US. While they may have qualified as a teacher, they may not hold a degree in physics, chemistry, mathematics, English or each of the subjects they are asked to teach. In Finland, for example, it is a requirement of the Masters candidates for a teaching degree that they have completed a Bachelors degree with a major in the subject they intend to teach. Finland is unusual in this regard, though other countries are now following their lead – e.g. in Shanghai, 90% of teacher education focuses on mastering the subject the person will teach[45].

9. The key curriculum design assumption of most school systems are based around "batch processing of students" – classes and year groupings, as opposed to individualized or personalized instruction. They also assume a model of instruction which is largely teacher led and directed as opposed to learner led and centred.

10. Securing key literacy outcomes is a secondary objective of the curriculum. It is possible to graduate from many school systems with a low level of literacy (below Level 3 literacy)[46], as evidenced by statistics concerning adult literacy in developed nations.

Schools, in addition to all other expectations, are expected to teach a range of knowledge and skills which is considerable, demanding and involve a high risk of failure. Given these conditions, schools have done (in general) remarkably well. But they are feeling the strain.

Two particular issues are creating concerns. The first is a desire to change the curriculum – to focus more on higher level competencies and skills rather than just mastery - and to do so over so-called 21st century skills (more on that later). The second is the speed at which knowledge is changing.

Teachers are concerned about the changing curriculum since it takes time for them and their students to adjust to change, especially ones in which they have not been involved. Changing curriculum often involves changing mind-sets.

Parents, teachers and students are concerned that the speed at which knowledge is changing – new discoveries in biology, the emergence of new sciences in nanotechnology and molecular chemistry, our emerging understanding of climate science – all require constant attention to the appropriate literature; something which teachers are not generally given time to pursue.

The result is often that we are offering instruction which relates to dated knowledge and understanding, much to the dissatisfaction of the teachers themselves.

The School 'Jigsaw'

Schools may have other functions: opening their doors early and closing late to provide shelter and care for students while their responsible adults work, for example – but these eight key functions are the ones that matter most.

Look at them on this conceptual map. The challenge is that we expect teachers and teacher administrators to undertake these functions; many of which require specialized knowledge, understanding and skills which teachers do not possess.

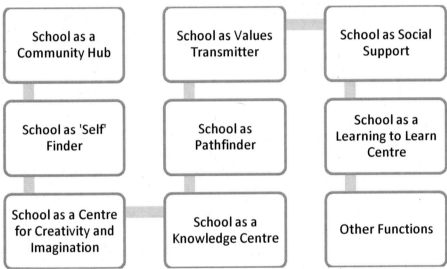

Figure Five: Mind Map of the Key Elements in the Work of the School

It is for this reason that schools are regarded as permanently failing organizations – while they may succeed in some aspects of their work, it is not possible for every school to achieve every desirable outcome in each of the key domains above all of the time.

Permanently failing organizations have several key characteristics [47]. One is that old organizations continue to survive, despite evidence of poor performance; small rural schools being a very good example[48]. A second is that new kinds of schools and educational organizations rarely survive (e.g. Risinghill) and are generally quickly assimilated. Third, attempts to change such organizations fail since the competing interests of stakeholders act to create paralysis associated with attempts at permanent change: new targets or processes are quickly assimilated and repurposed so that they resemble 'acceptable' activity for the organization that knows how to survive change attempts. More recent work on permanently failing organizations, based on cases [49], confirms the view that "sustained underperformance was not the outcome of deliberate or intentional actions in the part of organizational actors but that it was rather the unintended result of as myriad of practices from actors both inside and outside the organization". It also appears from this same work that the perpetual hope of what might be termed "outcome transformation" sustains these same actors, despite several decades of evidence that such hope appears a delusion. We can also conceptualize this issue in terms of systems archetypes[50] – repeated and known patterns of systems behaviour - that define what is happening in school systems: that the dominant archetype appears to be "the tragedy of the commons"[51].

School systems can be regarded as permanently failing organizations when a listing of the competing expectations of different stakeholders is taken together. Schools, as we have seen, are now:

Fighting for external resources while internal resources are wasted

(a) engines of the human capital strategy for a jurisdiction – a labour market organization;
(b) centres for the care and social well being of young people – a social service;
(c) a centre for health and wellness, especially in tackling key diseases such as obesity and childhood diabetes – a health care organization;
(d) a place engaged in the development of citizenship and community engagement – a community centre;
(e) a place that can support the moral and social development of young people – a social values organization;
(f) a centre for the development of environmental responsibility; and
(g) a place where learning takes place.

While some see these as complementary roles for schools, they do in fact compete, as resources are scarce and the competencies required to fulfill all of these expectations are not available in all schools. Thus school systems fail to meet the expectations of one or more (and in many cases, most) stakeholders.

School systems also often fail to meet educational expectations. Secondary schools, for example, generally remain organized around a particular structure of the school day with 45-50 minute "periods" (sometimes double periods occur) in which "subjects' are taught. As demands for content grow, so does the number of objectives for each curriculum area. Teachers have less and less creative time. As curriculum changes, students have little say in any of this activity, and parents have some role to play (differing by system), but are generally marginalized. Various educational reform and change attempts are made cyclically (in some school systems, in alternate years), often, as a study of literacy

Need for feedback loops.

*high achievement on tests
becomes the desired yield*

performance over thirty years in Britain showed, with little or no impact[52]. Schools are required to subject themselves in many countries to what has become known as "high stakes testing", which have the effect of corrupting learning and generally obfuscating some of the key challenges faced by the school as evidenced by the Cambridge University Primary School Review[53]– the test results, rather than "real learning" become the focus for the work of the system. Even in educational terms, schools are permanently failing organizations – they do not meet the educational ambitions many have for them.

Refocusing the Work of the School

What is needed is a rethink of the position of the school in the community, and a redefinition of the function of schooling. If schools want to stop being permanently failing organizations, they need to stop trying to be all things to all people. They need to redefine the scope of their work and their competencies.

Key to the changed position of schools should be these six propositions:

1. **Proposition 1 - Schools are The Vehicle for Education of Young People**: Schools are the primary unit for the development of learning, creativity and imagination in the community for young people. They are the place students and staff identify with and they should be granted the necessary autonomy to manage the school effectively.

2. **Proposition 2 - Learning to Learn is the Primary Work of the School**: The work of the school should be focused upon developing a commitment to learning as a process, which requires the skills of design, critical thinking, understanding knowledge, and managing knowledge.

What

What

creative thinkers resilient learners

creating resilient learners

3. **Proposition 3 - Problem Based Work Should be the Primary Focus for The Majority of Learning**: Working on wicked problems and projects is the primary way of developing personal learning and team learning, as well as enabling creative problem solving and the mastery of key knowledge and skills.

What

4. **Proposition 4 - Teachers Should Facilitate Learning and Creativity – Others Should Perform Related Supports**: Teachers, acting as coaches, mentors, guides and instructors, should enable the learning and creativity work of the school. Other professionals – social workers, psychologists, rehabilitation therapists, health professionals and law enforcement – should perform related functions. Teachers cannot be all things to all people.

How

5. **Proposition 5 - Learning Assessment and Public Assurance Provide the Accountability Framework for the Schools' Work:** Testing of all children at key stages so as to demonstrate 'systems' performance does not provide an evidence based framework for helping each student. Schools need to undertake daily, weekly, monthly, quarterly assessment of every learner according to the rubrics of the activities the students are engaged in. Schools within a district should have a framework for public assurance, similar to the triple bottom line framework of corporations, so that value for money can be assessed for all schools.

How

6. **Proposition 6 - Schools Should, as Often as is Practical and Possible, See Learning as Personal and Individual Rather than Batched and Graded:** The key challenge for the school is to engage every student in the pursuit of active, meaningful learning. Grouping students makes

How

economic sense only if each learner in the group is engaged.

The balance of this book is made up of most of these propositions, but the first proposition needs to be addressed here.

In the industrial model of education, schools within a jurisdiction were organized in regional divisions (School Board, Local Education Authorities), and each jurisdiction appointed an educational leader (Director of Education, Superintendent of Schools) to 'oversee' and 'control' the school system. Such a design was all a part of the Taylorism of management in the inter-war and post-war years.

We are now in the twenty first century, and the evidence from years of work on school effectiveness and value-added show clearly that the culture of each school (as shaped by its educational leadership and engagement with the community) is the primary variable having an impact on student performance. While others can support such a culture, they can also disrupt it. What is needed is for our systems to recognize that schools are different – no one size fits all – and that they need to be provided both the means and autonomy to operate effectively in the community and context in which they are placed.

This in turn requires school based decision making, an ability to manage school based budgets and a great degree of flexibility in day to day operations – all within the framework of an agreed understanding of the purpose of schooling and the expected performance of students within the school, given the characteristics of the incoming student population. The OECD PISA analysis makes this point very clearly, for there is a significant and substantial difference in outcomes (especially in science) between those schools who are able to select their own teachers and those who have teachers allocated to them from a central pool. Indeed, the quality of teachers and their collective ability to build a culture that is passionate about performance and resilient in the face of challenge or change is the key determinant of educational outcomes.

If schools are disabled from collective capacity building and a District or Local Education Authority continually disrupts the progress a school makes to creating an effective culture of high performance, then the school will continue to be permanently failing.

The Challenge

The first chapter ended with a challenge and so, too, does this one. The challenge is to build an effective system in which schools can create their culture and focus on; learning to learn; creative problem solving; and the development of knowledge and skills using high quality teachers chosen by the school.

A related challenge is for teachers to stop doing work best left to other professionals and for the investments to be made to permit this to happen. Teachers are challenged enough by the demands of teaching and learning, and they are not trained as social workers, psychologist, remedial therapists, or any other professions.

Chapter 3: What Do Students Need to Learn?

"In times of change, learners inherit the Earth, while the learned find themselves beautifully equipped to deal with a world that no longer exists..."

Eric Hoffer

Introduction

[handwritten note: resilient students are prepared for anything because they have created connections.]

Many school systems and schools are engaged in the implementation of curriculum programs aimed at the development of 21st century skills. These skills, many of which are not at all new to schools or to education (some can be linked to the Socratic method) are not new or the only skills needed for the current age. They are generally captured in the diagram below, taken from The Alliance for 21st Century Skills.

Digital Age Literacy

- Basic Scientific, Economic and Technological Literacies
- Visual and Information Literacies
- Multicultural Literacies and Global Awareness

Inventive Thinking

- Adaptability, Managing Complexity & Self Direction
- Curiosity, Creativity and Risk Taking
- Higher Order Thinking and Sound Reasoning

Engaged, Informed and Skilled Citizens

Effective Communication

- Teaming, Collaboration & Interpersonal Skills
- Personal, social and civic responsibility
- Interactive communication

High Productivity

- Prioritizing, planning and managing for results
- Effective use of real world tools
- Ability to produce relevant, high quality products
- Ability to innovate through continuous improvement

Figure Six: The 21st Century Skills Framework

Many take for granted the 21st century skills framework and assume it all makes sense. This is unfortunate. The framework needs systematic challenge, as many educators have pointed out[54]. Some, such as Sir Ken Robinson, see this approach to learning as a distraction from the real challenges – challenges which he clearly outlined in his major report for the British government – known as the Robinson Report (1999) *All Our Futures – Creativity, Culture and Education* [55] . He has also undertaken several presentations on the theme of this document[56], all of which suggest that creativity and cultural education linked to critical thinking and the constructs and skills of design should be seen *as being as important* as maths and science at all stages of learning, both in terms of the personal value of formal learning and in terms of the economic benefit of such work. Yet many jurisdictions are focusing class time and resources on technology, maths and science at the expense of drama, dance, music, art, creative writing and other activities.

These areas of study are rich grounds for the development of so called 21st century skills, yet they are seen as "optional" activities rather than core in many school systems.

Other critiques of this 21st century skills framework see these skills as a way of repositioning much of the existing teaching agenda without making substantial changes to the nature of the process of learning. Schools could 'teach' these skills within the framework of existing curriculum and knowledge promotion – it is not really a major change. 21st century skills may not be that different in terms of the knowledge focus from 20th century skills, but the way in which we secure this knowledge and understanding (the pedagogy) may need to be very different.

Agree.

The emphasis on collaborative team based work, civic responsibility and global activity all suggest a renewed pedagogy.

There are several related challenges for teachers, learners and parents in connecting 21st century skills to the work of schools. Amongst them are:

1. The curriculum and the base of knowledge; skills in and of themselves are processes and approaches to the understanding of core subjects (mathematics, history, chemistry, social studies, language arts and so on). *How do 21st century skills relate to the traditional and established curriculum?*

2. Given that students are currently assessed in terms of curriculum knowledge and some limited skills, how can teachers and learners develop the ability to focus on both mastery of knowledge and skills? *What changes to assessment practices do we need to enable to facilitate the development of 21st century skills?*

3. Given the nature of the curriculum and related assessment practices, the 21st century skills framework is often taken to suggest that there is a need for a different approach to pedagogy; that fundamentally, 21st century skills require experiential learning. *What are the implications of the skills framework for the process of teaching and learning?*

4. Related to this last question is another. The degree to which learners feel engaged with their lessons and learning is known to be a critical determinant of learning outcomes, yet engagement is rarely measured. Given that not all students are engaged (some are engaged only tactically and others are disengaged, for example), *how can*

a focus on 21st century skills enable a significant and measurable increase in student engagement in their learning?

5. Parents and teachers also are concerned that a change of pedagogy will have an impact on the learning outcomes of students – some positive, some negative. For example, will the adoption of more project based learning and less formal teaching have a positive or negative impact on learning outcomes? The question here is *what is the evidence base for a change of teaching method?*

6. Finally, there are challenges about the place of technology in the process of learning and teaching. While it is apparent that technology has a place – it's part of the lives of many (though not all) learners and is at the heart of the economy – the adoption and effective use of technology by teachers appears problematic. Less than 50% of teachers appear to use technology appropriately and frequently, much of the technology in use is supportive and not transformative of traditional teaching, and the technology has little impact on learning outcomes. The question here is *what is the place of technology in the modern classroom?*

These questions, and others, are at the heart of the debate on education in Canada and the US, with several jurisdictions enacting new approaches in legislation and in strategy so as to facilitate the appropriate adoption of a 21st century skills approach to learning, supported by technology.

Policy Challenges

As an example of this last point, a paper by Jensen, Taylor and Fisher (2010)[57] implies a set of policy challenges with respect to the implementation of the agenda of 21st century skills, learning and technology in a specific jurisdiction: Ontario. These include:

1. **Social Equity** – Not all students in Ontario have access to broadband and not all students have ongoing access to technology or a supportive environment in which to use technology. Jensen et al rightly suggest (see page 11) that one policy consideration concerns equity: "..the role of ICT in the classrooms, in the context of 21st century skills, technology and learning, is arguably about providing access and scaffolding to students, *and thereby creating educationally equitable and socially just teaching and learning environments.*" (our emphasis)

2. **Return on Capital Employed (ROCE)** – technology is expensive when deployed across a complex educational system such as operates in Ontario. It is especially expensive when, as Jensen et al make clear, there is little evidence that the deployment of such technology has a sustainable impact either on student engagement or on learning outcomes. The policy issue here is the conditions under which schools will be able to purchase technology – what commitments will be made with respect to its adoption and use by teachers and the impacts such use will have on engagement, 21st century skills and learning outcomes?

3. **Assessment and Measurement** – Jensen et al skilfully point out that the assessment of 21st century skills and student engagement is neither systematic nor effective. What is not said is that many schools do not focus on such assessment

activity at all. The policy question here relates to the resources which need to be made available to encourage the systematic use of assessments for 21st century skills and student engagement. There is a danger that "what gets measured, gets done" or, more accurately, "what doesn't get measured, we talk about a lot".

4. **The Policy Scaffolding with Respect to Differentiated Instruction** – the combination of a focus on 21st century skills and technology provides the opportunity for differentiated instruction (called personalized learning by many[58]). Jensen *et al*, in their concluding paragraph, also indicate that this is a challenge:

> "...the 21 century skills and learning made possible by new technologies represent a fundamental challenge to the individuated yet homogenizing systems for assessing and measuring learning that are currently in place." (page 19)

The current model of schooling is largely based on year-based age groups having limited choice over both what they learn and who teaches. Other jurisdictions – Finland, for example – have moved to a course credit system for high school which gives students choices over what they learn, when they learn and who will teach. Other systems are developing approaches to flexible learning based on course credits which can be negotiated by students or given for work-based learning;

community based learning or unique offerings by teachers. The constraints here are: (a) the requirements for graduation from a grade or high school; (b) the availability of accredited instruction; and (c) the availability of appropriate technologies to support this learning. There are also physical constraints in the design of schools (personal spaces for learning are at a premium).

5. **The Nature of Curriculum** – In some school systems, the number of curriculum objectives to be 'mastered' in a given grade inhibits the imaginative exploration of 21st century skills and limits the opportunity for teachers to leverage technology. In one school jurisdiction, Grade 7 students are expected to master 1,326 learning objectives within the school year. Teachers and students are trying to 'cover' the curriculum. What changes need to be made to the curriculum expectations for students at all grades so that 21st century skills and related pedagogy can be practiced effectively? Singapore has adopted the philosophy "teach less, learn more". Maybe there is a lesson here for us all.

6. **The Balance of the Curriculum** – What is the place of studies which promote creativity, communication and collaboration and critical thinking – drama, dance, music, art, for example – versus maths, science and technology? If the work of many scholars are to be believed, these domains of learning are equally important as a foundation for the creative classes which will shape the new economy[59]. While the US is reducing the amount of time schools spend on the arts so as to strengthen a

focus on technology, maths and science, it is ignoring the growing importance of creative design and imagination in the process of innovation; central to the economic development of a nation. As Canada's productivity and competitiveness declines, for example, so the importance of innovation increases; the arts are a critical vehicle for enabling the development of innovation skills and competencies.

7. **Teacher Professional Development** – Jensen et al point in a focused way to the lack of preparation teachers have for the use of technology as a cornerstone of their pedagogy. Using technology, for most teachers, is "an add on", not core. Adoption rates for technology vary between school districts and within schools, but rarely exceed 50% of teachers (even after significant investments in PD). What are the policy implications of this for the funding of initial teacher education and for the investments made in professional development?

The good news is that they are not alone in seeking to tackle exactly these challenges. New Brunswick and Alberta, for example, are in the midst of major reforms of their school systems based on these same set of issues [60] as are many jurisdictions in the US and Europe. Shared insights and learning from others, especially with the assistance of the OECD, is possible. The Alberta Teachers' Association (ATA) has developed a substantial partnership with schools and educational leaders in Finland and Alberta so as to leverage these opportunities for partnership[61]. Recotore

But these are challenging fiscal times. A concern will be the perception that the changes made for sound educational reasons are being driven by fiscal concerns; always a problem. A strong alliance between teacher unions, school boards, educational administrators and government is essential if success is to be achieved in making curriculum change meaningful in the experience of learners.

One final point, not addressed in the Jensen et al paper: Personalised learning is the challenge to meet more of the needs of more students more fully than has been achieved in the past; it is concerned with a transformation of education and schooling that is fit for citizens in the 21st century[62].

We should not be distracted from other critical issues by a focus on personalization empowered by emerging technologies. Issues engendered by the pervasive digital connectivity of young people and society are important if we hope to achieve a healthy balance in our society. There is a growing call for studies on the physiological effect of digital technologies and new media on children's brain development: a neuroscience of children and media [63]. Based on this concern, we should consider the personal cost to 8–18 year olds who, on average, spend 10 hours and 45 minutes a day exposed to media, including television, video and music [64]. We also need to listen to the concerns of the Canadian Paediatric Society, documented in their recent policy recommendation of no screen time for children under two years of age and a maximum of two hours for children older than two[65].

Finally, we should be mindful of the need for 'stillness' in a digital age where a kind of solitude that refreshes and restores a person is valued. Stillness is a particular concern that distinguished Professor Sherry Turkle, Director of the Massachusetts Institute of Technology (MIT) Initiative on Technology and Self, argues is essential to identity formation and healthy adolescent development in the 21st century. As Turkle speculates:

> "If we identify our need for stillness as something that is part of our human purposes, we will find ways to bring it back into our lives. If we only get excited about what technology makes easy, we will say that this is a kind of...18th century completely passé thing and that it is not essential."

Part of K-12 education should be to give students a place for this kind of stillness, because I don't think that the rest of their lives is making it easy for them [66]. The key challenge is to make teaching and learning mindful [67] and to enable learners to become more mindful as a result of their learning. This requires the development of intentionality and a commitment to owning decisions and actions, as well as the development of skills[68].

The Delores Framework

Few argue that the curriculum in place at the turn of this century in the majority of schools in the developed world should be the curriculum in place now. Knowledge changes, and the needs of society change. Curriculum should reflect these changes and be a vehicle for enabling students to develop the knowledge, skills and understanding they require to move forward as citizens, workers and members of families. The 21st century skills framework is the one that is currently receiving a great deal of traction amongst school administrators and ministers of education, but it is not the only framework.

Jacques Delores, the former Prime Minister of France, has worked with UNESCO to develop a framework which has power and focus[69]. Known as the "four pillars", it sees these four domains as the core work of the school[70]:

- **Learning to Know** - This type of learning is concerned less with the acquisition of structured knowledge than with the mastery of learning as a process. It aims to develop the pleasure that can be derived from understanding, knowledge and discovery. That aspect of learning is typically enjoyed by researchers, but good teaching can help everyone to enjoy it. Such a focus encourages greater intellectual curiosity, sharpens the critical faculties and enables people to develop their own independent judgements on the world around them. From that point of view, all must have a chance to receive an appropriate science education and become friends of science throughout their lives – science will be a dominant focus for innovation and change in the robotic-biotechnology age we are now experiencing.

- **Learning to Do** - This type of learning is most often associated with the occupational training: how do we adapt education so that it can equip people to do the types of work needed in the future? It emphasizes the knowledge component of tasks, even in industry, as well as the importance of services in the economy. The future of our economies hinges on their ability to turn advances in knowledge into innovations that will generate new businesses and new jobs. "Learning to do" can no longer mean what it did when people were trained to perform a very specific physical task in a manufacturing process. Skill training therefore has to evolve and become more than just a means of imparting the knowledge needed to do a more or less routine job.

- **Learning to Live Together** – As the global war for talent intensifies and the developed economies rely increasingly on immigration to sustain their well-being, tensions will arise over access to employment, wealth and other issues. These are already seen in terms of tensions in Britain between immigrant workers and "British" unemployed, between people of different faiths (for example, Muslims) throughout the European union and native Europeans, between ethnic groups within communities. Living together is no longer something we can take for granted – it needs to be worked at. Conflict management and multicultural understanding should no longer be optional topics of conversation, but should be a focus for educational systems.

- **Learning to Be** - Education should contribute to every person's complete development; mind and body, intelligence, sensitivity, aesthetic appreciation and spirituality. All people should receive in their childhood and youth an education that equips them to develop their own independent, critical way of thinking and judgement so that they can make up their own minds on the best courses of action in the different circumstances in their lives. As a means of personality development and growth, education should be a highly individualized process and at the same time an interactive social experience.

These four pillars, very different from the four pillars associated with 21st century skills, provide a basis for a humanistic, values-driven education which is not temporal in the sense of changing as the skills needs in the economy change. The Delores framework is robust and likely to stand the test of time. The challenge is that it is at a very high level. What is needed is a translation of this high level view of the purpose of schooling to a more concrete statement of what students should learn.

The Person Focused Learning Agenda

Let us then offer an outline of what the learner who leaves school should be able to do, using the Delores framework and the 21st century skills framework as our starting points. This 'prescription' will still be at a high level, but professional teachers working with curriculum specialists can translate it into concrete work for classrooms.

1. **Learning to Know. A learner leaving K-12 education should be able to:**

    a. Have a passion for curiosity.
    b. Read and understand communications at Level 3 literacy or higher[71].
    c. Demonstrate the skills of critical thinking and knowledge assessment.
    d. Understand and be able to analyze systems and be developing the skills of systems thinking and analysis.
    e. Know and use the processes of design and engage in project work using design principles.

f. Be able to gather, arrange, codify and assess knowledge materials from a variety of sources and assess their veracity.

g. Understand and use the process of problem finding and solving.

h. Be able to explore creative use of media, art, music, drama, dance and other fine arts as a route to learning.

i. Be able to undertake independent study.

j. Be able to engage in team based problem-solving.

k. Be able to communicate in writing, verbally and using digital media to share their findings and understanding in a way that persuades an appropriate audience that they have understood a complex problem.

l. Understand and demonstrate in practice the process by which they master a skill and understand a body of knowledge or a set of principles.

m. Be able to engage in cross-disciplinary study.

n. Be able to critically review and analyze scientific reports and test accounts of this science which appear in the media.

o. Be able to use social networks so as to support their problem solving and critical thinking.

p. Be able to specify a problem that needs solving and design a process by which the problem can be understood, solution options assessed and a strategy for change proposed.

In short, they will develop the skills and competencies required for life-long learning and critical-reflective citizenship.

2. **Learning to Do. A learner leaving K-12 education should be able to:**

    a. Demonstrate Level 3 literacy and the equivalent skill in numeracy and the core understanding of science.

    b. Develop visual literacy and an ability to discern patterns.

    c. Manage their finances and understand financial literacy.

    d. Demonstrate mastery of life-skills, including the skills of personal mastery, teamwork and emotional intelligence.

    e. Demonstrate the ability to complete a core set of skills related to a trade or occupation of their choice – completing the initial stages of apprenticeship, trade or professional skill during their high school (secondary school) years.

    f. Demonstrate mastery of the key skills associated with the work of the core knowledge disciplines – biology, physics, chemistry, mathematics, language arts, social science, history, environmental studies.

    g. Demonstrate customer service skills and the skills associated with dealing with difficult people.

    h. Demonstrate mastery of digital technologies for social networking, managing work processes, presenting ideas, finding and managing knowledge, collaboration and problem-solving.

3. **Learning to Live Together**. A learner leaving K-12 education should be able to:

a. Describe and document their own values and personal philosophy.

b. Understand how their behaviour appears to others – their behavioural style.

c. Demonstrate empathy, warmth and genuineness in their interactions with others, especially those whose cultural backgrounds and experiences are different from their own.

d. Demonstrate their ability to interact with persons whose belief systems are different from their own and show respect, understanding and empathy when doing so.

e. Be able to recognize conflict conditions and use strategies for resolving conflict.

f. Be able to agree to disagree without losing respect for the person with whom they disagree.

g. Understand how disputes arise in science (e.g. in relation to climate change, stem cell research, ethics) and the mechanisms used to settle such disputes.

h. Using the knowledge and understanding of scientific disputation, be able to understand conflict resolution in other disciplines – especially economics, politics, social science.

i. Understand the bias in media reporting of events.

j. Have a strong and demonstrable sense of civic responsibility.

4. **Learning to Be. A learner leaving K-12 education should be able to:**

   a. Describe their own values and beliefs and indicate areas where they are seeking to improve their understanding of their 'self'.
   b. Be able to reflect on their own actions and thoughts in a reflective and developmental way.
   c. Understand their strengths and limitations as a person and develop an agenda for self-improvement.
   d. Be able to assess and take risks.
   e. Manage their fitness levels through healthy eating and exercise.
   f. Manage their stress levels in ways which are appropriate to their psychological profile – relaxation for anxiety stress or high energy activities for boredom stress, or a combination of both.
   g. Be able to effectively engage in team based activities.
   h. Have strong inter-personal skills.
   i. Be able to manage failure, rejection and disappointment.
   j. Develop the capacities for resilience.

Additional outcomes could no doubt be suggested that would be highly desirable, but these are the core of what our young people require for responsible citizenship, productive work and social and personal well-being. They also embody 21st century skills, in so far as these have been articulated, but go beyond the economically desirable outcomes from learning to place them in the context of the person.

These outcomes are also consistent with the multiple-intelligences which Howard Gardner has urged educationists to keep at the forefront of their thinking in designing strategies for teaching and learning[72]. These intelligences include:

- **Linguistic intelligence** involves sensitivity to spoken and written language, the ability to learn languages, and the capacity to use language to accomplish certain goals. This intelligence includes the ability to effectively use language to express oneself rhetorically or poetically; and language as a means to remember information. Writers, poets, lawyers and speakers are among those that Howard Gardner sees as having high linguistic intelligence.
- **Logical-mathematical intelligence** consists of the capacity to analyze problems logically, carry out mathematical operations, and investigate issues scientifically. In Howard Gardner's words, it entails the ability to detect patterns, reason deductively and think logically. This intelligence is most often associated with scientific and mathematical thinking.
- **Musical intelligence** involves skill in the performance, composition, and appreciation of musical patterns. It encompasses the capacity to recognize and compose musical pitches, tones, and rhythms. According to Howard Gardner musical intelligence runs in an almost structural parallel to linguistic intelligence.
- **Bodily-kinaesthetic intelligence** entails the potential of using one's whole body or parts of the body to solve problems. It is the ability to use mental abilities to

coordinate bodily movements. Howard Gardner sees mental and physical activity as related.

- **Spatial intelligence** involves the potential to recognize and use the patterns of wide space and more confined areas.
- **Interpersonal intelligence** is concerned with the capacity to understand the intentions, motivations and desires of other people. It allows people to work effectively with others. Educators, salespeople, religious and political leaders and counsellors all need a well-developed interpersonal intelligence.
- **Intrapersonal intelligence** entails the capacity to understand oneself, to appreciate one's feelings, fears and motivations. In Howard Gardner's view it involves having an effective working model of ourselves, and to be able to use such information to regulate our lives.
- **Naturalist intelligence** enables human beings to recognize, categorize and draw upon certain features of the environment. It 'combines a description of the core ability with a characterization of the role that many cultures value'

The intention of these different intelligences is to shape the design of learning in such a way as it enables the many facets of the student to be explored and developed during their K-12 journey.

You will notice that, while there are some references to specific subjects taught in schools, the focus is on personal outcomes – what it is that the person will be able to do, whether they are passionate about art, science, music, history, literature, dance, chemistry or mathematics. In the next chapter we will look more carefully at how these outcomes can be achieved, but it needs to be clear here that the traditional subjects taught in schools in engaging ways can all be vehicles for these outcomes. That is, this is not a set of proposals to throw "the baby out with the bathwater", but to see the work of schools in terms of these outcomes, whatever the specific learning activity may be.

Put simply: while one set of objectives associated with the teaching of, say, Shakespeare, may be to understand the meaning of the play and the social context in which the play was written, another set of objectives in this same work would be to connect the meaning of the play to the person of the student – what meaning does this have for him or her and how does this play help them understand their place in the world?

The Challenge

The challenge implied by this agenda for learning is to rethink how we engage learners in a way that achieves the outcomes outlined while maintaining a focus on their self and their needs: how do we personalize and make meaningful this agenda, given their interest, skills, levels of support and intentions for their future? A related challenge is how to reduce the content of the curriculum – the number of specific learning objectives related to the subject matter – and increase the meaning of that learning. Not easy challenges.

Needs & Yields.

Chapter 4: What Should Teachers Do?

"The best way to predict the future is to design it"

-*Buckminster Fuller*

Introduction

The key to a great school is the quality of teaching learners experience at the school. Great teachers make a great deal of difference – they engage and enable students and ennoble the work of learning in the process. Elizabeth MacDonald and Dennis Shirley speak to this eloquently in their book *The Mindful Teacher*[73]. There they describe the seven synergies of mindful teachers –the ways of working which make a difference to learners. These are:

1. **Open Mindedness** – mindful teachers engage with their students, parents and community in finding relevant and meaningful opportunities to connect ideas, learning resources, their own and their students' interests so as to continuously connect learning to the minds of students.
2. **Loving and Caring** – they demonstrate a genuine care and concern and appropriate affection for their learners and the knowledge they work with.
3. **Professional Expertise** – they demonstrate daily, through their knowledge and processes, their expertise as teachers and as coaches, mentors and guides.
4. **Authentic Alignment** – they are genuinely and warmly engaged and aligned with the work of the school and give meaning to this work for students.

5. **Integrative and Harmonizing** – they enable students and others to make connections, see patterns, think in terms of systems and promote an understanding of the connectedness of curriculum.

6. **Collective Responsibility** – rather than relying on high stakes testing, mindful teachers understand that they have a responsibility to evaluate and enable learning and to understand where a learner is in their journey towards mastery of a specific subject. While one teacher may have a 'piece' of this puzzle – collectively all who teach a student are better placed than any one individual teacher to "assess" and determine next steps to support the student. Quality teachers not only understand this collective responsibility, but they act accordingly.

7. **Stopping** – quality mindful teachers stop and take time to critically reflect on their work. They also take time to take care of themselves, not just occasionally, but daily. They engage in what is known as "reflective practice". That is, they work at their own "inner balance" to be better able to support students in a mindful way.

In a variety of activities which these authors and others have conducted since the publication of this book in 2009, teachers report that "stopping" and finding balance for themselves is the most difficult of these seven synergies for them to consistently practice. They also report that the pressure of the volume of learning objectives which are subject focused – 267 objectives for the science curriculum in Grade 7 in Alberta, for example - makes integration, harmonizing and authentic alignment difficult, especially when the class size grows and there are several students with special needs in the classroom.

Other work supports the position taken by MacDonald and Shirley. For example, Mindy Kornhaber and her colleagues at the Project SUMIT (Schools Using Multiple Intelligences Theory) have examined the performance of a number of schools and concluded that there have been significant gains in respect of third party assessment scores (e.g. SATs), parental participation, and discipline (with the schools themselves attributing this to the work on multiple intelligence). They have identified the following markers that characterize schools with some success in implementing practices that attend to multiple intelligences theory[74]:

[handwritten: Justification of diversity in the classroom]

- **Culture:** support for diverse learners and hard work. Acting on a value system which maintains that diverse students can learn and succeed, that learning is exciting, and that hard work by teachers and students is necessary.
- **Readiness:** awareness-building for implementing the multiple-intelligence (MI) approach. Building staff awareness of MI and of the different ways that students learn.

[handwritten: Projects that tap into student diversity]

- **Tool**: MI is a means to foster high quality work. Using MI as a tool to promote high quality student work rather than using the theory as an end in and of itself. Such work can be individual work by a student, project work by a team of students or the work of a class as a whole.
- **Collaboration**: informal and formal exchanges. Sharing ideas and constructive suggestions by the staff in formal and informal exchanges.
- **Choice**: meaningful curriculum and assessment options. Embedding curriculum and assessment in activities that are valued both by students and the wider culture.

[handwritten: ensures that diversity of learners in honoured and fulfilled.]

- **Arts:** Employing the arts to develop children's skills and understanding within and across disciplines.

The multiple intelligences themselves also provide a good focus for reflection. Arguably, informal educators have traditionally been concerned with the domains of the interpersonal and the intrapersonal, with a sprinkling of the intelligences that Howard Gardner identifies with the arts. Looking to naturalist linguistic and logical-mathematical intelligences could help enhance their practice.

Ten assumptions inform this chapter. These are:

1. There is a strong link between the quality of teaching and student performance.
2. Quality teaching is a function of; training and professional development; day to day collective support; and instructional leadership within the school and across the profession.
3. Contrary to the popular belief that a teacher is 'king or queen' in their classroom, the mindful teacher is most effective when they are part of a collective team working to ensure that learning for students in their school is an engaging and meaningful experience. Quality teachers do more than instruct; they coach, guide, mentor, cajole, challenge and enable.
4. Schools which develop a collective capacity for quality teaching are more likely to retain these teachers than those who do not do so.
5. Quality teachers create as well as deliver – they use their own knowledge, resources and networks to create

meaningful learning experiences which students find engaging and link these to the 'required' curriculum.

6. Quality teachers need time to stop and find their own balance.

7. Quality teachers work with the person we call "the student" – they don't teach subjects, they enable the development of individuals through their teaching.

8. Quality teachers understand the nature of teaching as a process – they are reflective practitioners. They also engage in the active pursuit of best and next practices so as to maintain the freshness of their understanding of teaching and learning as a processes.

9. Quality teachers inspire learning and encourage a commitment for lifelong learning.

10. Teaching should be regarded as a difficult profession to enter and one that few want to leave – especially once they see the impact that quality teaching can have on the minds and behaviour of students and the community in which they live.

These may appear to some as radical suggestions, especially in some jurisdictions where teaching is not seen as a full profession and where systematic attempts have been made to de-professionalize the work of teachers.

Securing Quality Teachers

Before we can talk about the process of teaching and the engagement of learners, we need to look at how teachers come to be teachers and what it takes to sustain a quality teacher over the course of their career. While some teachers are naturally gifted at their craft, most develop the skill through training, professional development, professional networking and practice.

Teacher education programs in some jurisdictions are not difficult to get into, but they should be. Standards for admission to such programs should be as high as for engineers, doctors and lawyers. Indeed, in those countries which lead the PISA performance tables, the requirements for admission into teacher education programs are generally difficult and demanding. Finland, for example, requires those entering such programs to complete a Bachelors degree with a major in the subject they are to teach and to complete a Masters level program before they enter the profession. The competition for places in teacher education in Finland is fierce[75]. This is also the case in Japan, which has had high standards for entry into teacher education since the days of the Meiji Restoration, over a century ago. Shanghai is systematically increasing entry standards each year and Singapore is focused on ensuring that only quality candidates are admitted[76].

In the US, students entering teacher education programs score low on SATs. A College Board study conducted in 2008 showed that those students who indicated that education was to be their college or university program major, they were in the bottom third of all college and university applicants on SAT's – some 57 points below the national average[77].

Further, the nature of teacher education is often seen as problematic. The late Chris Gonnet, Superintendent of Schools in Grande Prairie Public Schools (Alberta, Canada) developed an apprenticeship program for those who had graduated from teacher education programs so that they would develop some of

interesting

the key skills of classroom management, discipline, flexible and creative teaching which were not taught (or not taught effectively) during teacher education programs at university or college. Other jurisdictions have done the same. As the Professoriate in universities are rewarded not by the effectiveness of their teaching in terms of the impact of their trained teachers on schools and student performance, but by how much they publish and the scale of research grants they secure, the practice of teaching is increasingly less attractive than researching the failure of schools to teach.

One barrier to entry to the profession for the most able college and university bound students is the compensation package afforded to teachers. For Singapore, the Minister of Education has suggested that the key strategy for any government seeing education as the cornerstone of its future must be to "take compensation as an issue off the table"[78]. In the US, the average salary of a teacher is $30,377US – some $15,000 below that of a registered nurse or a beginning accountant. Average salaries of workers holding a four year degree across all professions in the US are some 50% higher than teachers' average salary[79]. While the public look to the long vacation periods teachers secure and to what they perceive as the hours of work (actual hours are substantially higher than public guesstimates), teaching is seen by many as a well paid profession. Not only is it not, is also a highly stressful one.

Until we find an approach to raising the quality of initial teacher education, our students will suffer and our schools will continue as permanently failing organizations.

Developing and Supporting Teachers

Once appointed, teachers need supports and investment of these kinds to sustain quality teaching:

1. **Novice teachers need coaching, guidance and mentoring from experienced teachers**. No amount of preparation can prepare a beginning teacher for the work of the classroom, the demands of students, the complex interaction with parents and caregivers and the complexity of educational reporting. Nor does initial teacher education prepare teachers well for the rigours of the curriculum and the demands of the profession. Counselling and helping are key to retention.

2. **All teachers need professional development**. This development needs to focus on the skills of enhancing student engagement and the enrichment of the learning process as well as on the development of knowledge and understanding of the disciplines which the teacher is asked to teach. Developments in all fields occur rapidly – teachers need to be cognisant of these developments so that their students receive a current education. Textbooks are dated by the time of publication – teachers need time to keep up.

3. **Teachers need time for collaborative learning design and lesson planning.** As the specification of what should be taught offered by the jurisdiction becomes 'lean', teachers should be expected to do more of the design of the learning experiences and be closely involved with the development of appropriate pedagogy associated with their discipline. They need to be designers of learning and learning encounters, not just deliverers. In some

jurisdictions, teachers within a discipline (e.g. mathematics, language arts, science) meet collaboratively monthly throughout the school year to focus on what works and best practice sharing. Others develop specialist associations or councils to support learning design and advanced teaching methodology. Whatever the model chosen, teachers need to make investments and to be enabled to do so in their pedagogical development. In adult training the assumption is generally made that each full day of training activity requires a full day and half of preparation. Should we not afford the same consideration to the teachers of our K-12 students?

4. **Teachers need support for the integration of technology into their designs for learning.** To some, technologies are intuitive. To many, however, technology represents a challenge. Teachers need not be afraid of technology, but the development of confidence and the ability to know how to leverage technology in the service of mindful teaching and purposive learning requires teachers to receive training and development.

5. **Teachers need encouragement to stop and reflect on their work.** Reflective practice requires time for reflection and time to recharge the batteries. Teachers are outstanding in giving of themselves to others – especially their students and their colleagues in the school – but are generally poor at giving time and support to themselves.

These five supports for teaching are not 'nice to haves' they are essential. Certified and qualified teachers should be required to demonstrate their continued professional development (CPD), should be required to receive supervision and support and should be paid for this work.

Recently, in one Canadian jurisdiction, the idea of shortening the school year for students so as to give more time for the work of professional development just outlined was found to be very problematic by school boards and by the politicians who act as gatekeepers the funding of the school system. "Students need more time in class, not less!" was the rallying cry of the opponents of this proposition. They are wrong on two counts:

First, students need high quality teachers offering mindful teaching which in turn requires these investments in the professional development of teaching. *requires resilient teachers.*

Second, there is no strong evidence to support the view that additional time on task leads to improved educational outcomes. Indeed, Finnish students spend a whole two years less in classrooms than their Canadian counterparts and perform better on standardized measures of attainment than Canadian students. The real argument here is whether society is willing to make the investments in the quality of teaching required to secure the outcomes for students which they profess to desire.

The Day to Day Work of Teaching

The foregoing describes the necessary conditions for quality teaching: the prerequisites for a high performing school system. But what should teachers do each day in the classroom? Two constructs need to be understood before this question can be answered. These are: (a) the nature of design; and (b) the nature of critical thinking.

The term "design" is important in this conversation. It is, according to Margolis and Buchanan (1995)[80], "the human power

feedback loops and meeting N & Y.

This is done through the creation of connections.

to conceive, plan, and realize products that serve human beings in the accomplishment of any individual or collective purpose". This term is used extensively when we speak of the "design of learning experiences" and embraces more specific models of design as a process in fields such as culinary arts, web design, video game design and simulation, interior design, architecture, marketing, sustainability, retail, packaging, set design in theatre, film, and so on. Many see design as moving beyond "innovation", which is a stage in the design process, and applying it to a wide array of challenges and opportunities, including those challenges which face communities [81]. More importantly, design provides a common core process and set of insights which inform a variety of communities of practice[82].

design is transferable across disciplines

Underlying the design process is "the management of constraints" [83] – designers have to meet the needs and expectations of clients or organizations, but they must also work within real constraints of resources, the laws of physics and biology, mathematics and science. Designers need to be both well informed and 'street smart'. Design is both a rigorous process and a creative one. It challenges individuals and teams to solve real world problems and, by doing so, create something new and inspiring; something that touches both hearts and minds. These are key requirements for workers in the twenty first century – an ability to use a design process to solve the next challenge that confronts them.

Need of skills

Given that there are challenges which communities face, there is a need to design processes which enable communities to respond creatively and imaginatively to these challenges, while recognizing within constraints. – A part of that process involves the simple question: What is it that schools can teach to develop

designers/critical thinkers/problem solvers are great at building connections and are thus more prepared

Teachers need to (A) encourage the capacity
for connection building by (B) tying learning
into real world needs and yields

the required skills and competencies for design and innovation
to be effective?

connection building

First, they can see design as a process at the heart of the
experience of learning and core to *all* curriculum domains – a
core skill and competency in which students need to be
successful in the twenty first century. This may seem like a bold
claim, but consider this: design involves both developing a `big
idea` that is appropriate to the challenge at hand, `landing` this
idea into a project and then executing this project, adapting to
circumstances and constraints en route, and then satisfying the
authentic customer or client for the challenge. Design is a life
skill.

meeting N & Yields

Second, teachers can help students find ways to harness the
power of learning with a focus on design so as to foster problem-
focused solution-finding linked to real world challenges and
authentic audiences. Challenge learners to solve a set of real
world problems that have real people wanting real solutions –
use this learning to secure authentic knowledge, engaged
learners, coverage of the skills and knowledge needed by the
curriculum at that stage of their development and enable the
learner to see the value of their learning through the
implementation of design. Problem based learning has a long
history and is widely used, especially in primary education.
What is needed is the extension of this approach to learning for
all learners, including those at colleges and universities. Access
to information, social networks and global mentoring supports
enables this in this century in a way that was hitherto impossible.

Third, they can connect the principles of design to the study of
different disciplines (philosophy, mathematics, biology, physics,

*different disciplines become the
context of the design projects*

history, social studies, language arts, etc). Rethinking curriculum in terms of both focus and process is essential as a means for rethinking schools and developing appropriate twenty first century learning – appropriate for the development of the human capital assets our communities need to solve "wicked problems". In doing so, they can help unleash creativity and imagination while at the same time delivering to the learning outcomes identified in the previous chapter.

The teaching of design has three components: thinking, making, and doing. To teach critical thinking and disciplined understanding, students need to have roots in the basic disciplines (science, mathematics, language arts, social studies, fundamentals of technology, philosophy) and be able to synthesize between these disciplines in an effective way.

= Create connections between.

Extensive and in-depth knowledge, at least during compulsory schooling, is less important than an in-depth understanding of the methodologies of these disciplines, the core knowledge required in these disciplines and an understanding of contemporary practices which make use of these disciplines[84].

Critical thinking skills, according to[85], are a complex array of ways of thinking which include analysis, inference, explanation, evaluation, and interpretation all conducted in a self-regulatory fashion. While these analytic and conceptual skills look abstract when presented here, they are in fact the bedrock of all disciplines. They can be taught, if approached systematically, through a variety of devices including (but not only by) a focus on science, mathematics, philosophy social studies, language arts and technology. However, critical thinking is not just a set of skills, it is also a *disposition*. Characteristics of a disposition to critical thinking), is demonstrated by the following attributes:

- inquisitiveness with regard to a wide range of issues
- concern to become and remain well-informed
- alertness to opportunities to use critical thinking
- trust in the processes of reasoned inquiry
- self-confidence in one's own abilities to reason
- open-mindedness regarding divergent world views
- flexibility in considering alternatives and opinions
- understanding of the opinions of other people
- fair-mindedness in appraising reasoning
- honesty in facing one's own biases, prejudices, stereotypes, or egocentric tendencies,
- prudence in suspending, making or altering judgments
- willingness to reconsider and revise views where honest reflection suggests that change is warranted.

Students' ypres need to meet the needs of othe

In terms of the 'making' component of critical thinking, students need to be challenged to produce tangible products, services or activities which are valued by others. Rather than simply producing essays, book reports, research posters for science – all of which have value – they should be required to work with community organizations on design challenges which will actually make a difference. For example, when a team of young students were asked to design a robot that would patrol levies and dams looking for cracks, these dispositions together with strong and effective teamwork and partnership with a group of adult mentors were fully on display. The 'making' was not just for class; it represented an opportunity to make a social contribution. This is also the case with other projects from the Galileo Educational Network[86], which has worked since 1998 with fifty thousand teachers around the world to develop meaningful learning challenges which not only develop skills, but enhance the disposition to see learning as a response to social challenges or opportunities.

'Doing' as a step in critical thinking, and also in the design process, represents the iterative process of offering a solution, testing that solution and then revising it in the light of evidence of performance, resource implications, constraint management, and customer or client feedback. This feedback can come from the teacher or others. It is important that as many 'real world' tests of the design process with different customer groups should occur across a student's school experience, since this will help the student understand the process of design.

Innovation illiteracy as assessed by a variety of instruments is now seen as a major challenge in economies seeking to secure jurisdictional advantage[87], can be combated in part through the development of a disposition to critical thinking coupled with the development of critical thinking skills, but also by the systematic pursuit of a design and creativity agenda across the curriculum[88]. There are a great many resources available to support this work, with several programs to develop the required skills for teachers now emerging (e.g. Buffalo State University offers graduate programs related to this work). Overcoming innovation illiteracy and promoting creativity, design and innovation should be seen as critical to the twenty first century human capital agenda.

the subjects are the tools to draw from in order to complete

Using "Wicked Problems" as the Focus for Learning

One vehicle for the teaching of critical thinking, design, innovation and creativity is to use authentic learning tasks or inquiry based learning as the core activity of schools – replacing subject based teaching, with learning activities that require disciplined knowledge, synthesis, critical thinking and design so that the response of the learners are not only appropriate, but based on the rigorous and disciplined development of knowledge and skills and a formalized rubric[89].

Needs

The core idea here is that real problems faced by communities, groups or individuals become the focal point through which learning occurs. While some of these problems may be simple – how do we know what CO_2 emissions emanate from the school and what can we do to reduce them – others may be much more complex and challenging. They may in fact be 'wicked' problems. The term "wicked problems" is used extensively in design and software development (e.g. Churchman, 1967 [90]). "Wicked problems" have certain common characteristics, according to Rittel and Melvin (1972)[91]. These include, according to Margolis & Buchanan (1995)[92]:

1. Wicked problems have no definitive formulation, but every formulation of a wicked problem conforms to the formulation of a solution.
2. Wicked problems have no stopping rules.
3. Solutions to wicked problems cannot be true or false, only good or bad.
4. In solving wicked problems, there is no exhaustive list of admissible operations or solutions.

5. For every wicked problem, there is always more than one possible explanation, with explanations depending on the *Weltanschauung* of the designer.
6. Every wicked problem is a symptom of a higher level (more wicked) problem.
7. No formulation and solution of a wicked problem has a definitive test.
8. Solving a wicked problem is a 'one shot' operation, with no room for trial and error.
9. Every wicked problem is unique.
10. Every wicked problem solver has no right to be wrong – they are fully accountable and responsible for their actions.

Such wicked problems, when based on genuine community or organizational needs, require learners to develop skills and competencies and also responsibility dispositions which should be characteristic of twenty first century learning and teaching. When the author of this book was training as a teacher, he was taught "never to ask a question to which you do not know the answer". By enabling learning through wicked problem solving he has learnt never to set a problem for which there is a known and solitary answer.

Many schools have already chosen to pursue problem based learning and wicked problems as a basis for a great deal of their learning activity. They understand the power of real life problems as tools for "carrying a range of curriculum and teaching options – the more `wicked`, the more the learning that is possible. The three short examples selected below are intended to be illustrative of the way in which a design focused process which uses critical thinking, innovation and creativity as the core methodologies for inquiry based learning could focus on meaningful community challenges and engage young people as being part of the solution to these challenges. Each of these requires student engagement, authenticity, rigour (as evidenced by both formative and summative assessment), engagement beyond the school, active exploration using appropriate technologies, a strong and meaningful connection to others (especially adults) with appropriate expertise, teamwork and elaborated communication as well as an element of fun and a lot of imagination.

Challenge	Focus for the Inquiry	Sample of Skills and Knowledge Required
Analyzing the Incidence of Childhood Obesity and Early Onset Diabetes of Family Members	• Understanding the links between food, exercise, smoking, social behaviour and health • Documenting the incidence of various stages of obesity amongst/diabetes in the age cohort in the community • Partnering with other schools globally to compare and contrast obesity and diabetes amongst the age cohort	• Some basic biology, nutrition, socio-economic geography, demographics, epidemiology, social history, comparative medical epidemiology • Range of measurement, recording and survey skills • Emotional intelligence and social sensitivity • Language arts and social studies (including historical approach to development of epidemics)
Advising the Community on Appropriate Adaptive	• Understanding the debate about climate change as a scientific challenge, a social challenge	• Understanding weather patterns and climate as different but related things • Ability to focus on

Responses to Climate Change	and a political challenge • Understanding regional scenarios for climate and weather systems over the lifetime of the student in their community • Looking at the impact of cooling and warming scenarios on water supplies, air quality, agriculture, health, biodiversity, power consumption and generation, migration patterns, etc from a regional / community perspective • Analyzing adaptation options and weighting them • Engaging others world-wide in this work	objective evidence and implications of evidence – generating.action plans based on scenarios • Understanding some basic physics, climatology, plant and animal biology and social studies • Analyzing economic options and understanding econometrics and social policy choice making • Being able to distinguish between rhetoric and reality in climate change policy and practice.
Proposing Services to end the social isolation and loneliness of older people – a 2008/9 project supported by	• Exploring how older people become involved, supported and reconnected to their neighborhoods and communities. • Does the key to addressing the problem of loneliness and	• Collecting and analyzing evidence and data about the socio-economic isolation of older persons in their community • Understanding social history, social policy and public health • Communication skills

| Calouste Gulbenkian Foundation and Glaxo Smith Kline in the UK and the Royal Society of Arts[93] | isolation lie with older people themselves? Will creating the opportunity for them to co-design their own outcomes lead to more appropriate services?
• Older people are a mine of information and experience. How can these be harnessed, valued and used?
• How can greater social cohesion between generations be fostered?
• What are the opportunities for new services, systems, networks and other solutions to counter isolation and support the health and wellbeing issues faced by the growing number of older people in society?
• – What evidence exists which might point towards viable solutions? | • Team skills
• Evaluative skills, in terms of evaluating data, status claims for knowledge
• Critical thinking and analysis
• Options evaluation and project management |

Figure Seven: Examples of Wicked Problem Based Learning

These examples are intended to illustrate the power of authentic wicked problems as a means for not only ensuring that system-wide curriculum expectations are met, but that, in doing so, students experience the fact that their knowledge and understanding can make a difference to a community. That is, rather than school being a preparation for life; school is a place where life is experienced to the full. Students develop a passion for learning based on rigour, depth of understanding and making a contribution. They also come to understand that action is not just what other people do; it is something each of us has a responsibility for. In this way, a focus on authentic wicked problems enables innovation to occur.

This work has often been misunderstood. The common misconception is that teachers abrogate their responsibilities for learning outcomes, since they shift from a role of instructor to a role of coach, guide and mentor[94]. Yet, as the evidence makes clear [95] teachers who engage their students in a process of discovery rooted in the need to master the core skills requirements of a jurisdiction (as opposed to the contents of a text book and the myriad of objectives which have found their way into a third party imposed curriculum), and in so doing understand the relevance of this learning to real world situations, achieve high level learning outcomes in both cognitive domains and emotional ones – emotional intelligence grows alongside knowledge and understanding[96].

Another misconception of the inquiry based approach is that it will be too difficult for students to chart their own course of learning; that they need the rigidity of a set verbatim curriculum, or that they are too intellectually immature for it to be effective.

Responding to this, Clifford & Marinucci, 2008 state:

> "Inquiry demands an orientation to what matters…Less rigorous approaches to inquiry, which privilege the children's questions and interests simply because they are the children's, can quickly degenerate into sentimental practice that shies away from thorny conversations about whether mistakes are being made or misconceptions overlooked…Students trained in the habits of inquiry have much less fear that making a mistake reveals their own personal ignorance and are much more interested in the quality of their thinking, part of which involves a commitment to rigor on behalf of the topic. Uncovering error becomes a way to learn".[97]

- pointing out that the rigour required to ensure that inquiry based learning is effective, is no less than the rigour to be found in serious scientific work or research in understanding social problems: rigour is the key.

For some time several organizations have been suggesting the idea of an X-Prize for Schools, based on a "wicked problem", such as schools working with local communities to reduce and sustain the reduction in water consumption in the community by 15% over the course of a year, in exchange for a significant prize that would benefit the whole school and the community – the creation and staffing of a technology design capacity within the school, for example. Schools compete, as they do in the Royal Society's Design Directions Challenge, but the impacts have to be demonstrated (rather than proposed) and have to be sustained over time. In such a case, schools become engines of creativity, design and innovation and students are recognized for their life contribution. This seems like a natural extension of a variety of initiatives underway, leveraging the experience of the X Prize Foundation (2009) and their offering of several X-prizes but also moving schools beyond the idea of preparing students for life and engaging them in solving real life challenges while at school.

The Role of Teachers and the Practice of Teaching

The conception of learning as the development of the skills of design and critical thinking and as vehicles to create authentic learning required to solve wicked problems for a genuine audience carries many implications for the nature of teaching. Teachers, in this formulation, move from "instructors" and the adult who is "in loco parentis" to being imagineers, facilitators, mentors, coaches, guides and brokers for knowledge workers in the community, as well as an instructor.

Teachers do still need to teach and 'instruct', but also need have access to more substantial resources to enable their teaching and instructional activities. Once they abandon text books and focus instead on learning as a process of finding relevant knowledge and the development of understanding so as to respond to wicked problems and challenges, teachers can achieve more. The teacher as instructor, coach, guide, mentor, facilitator and adult learner as well as problem solver is a powerful role; one that is imbued with professional skills and competencies. We refer to this conceptualization as teacher as "design consultant". Key teacher competencies for effective work for design based, problem focused, authentic learning include, but are not limited to:

teachers need to demonstrate the resiliency needed and the skills that they wish students to mirror.

- The setting of "wicked problems" with significant learning content and skills development as students work on authentic learning tasks for a real audience
- The ability to support inquiry as a basis for learning
- The understanding of design as a process at the heart of all learning activity
- The ability to develop both the skills of and disposition towards critical thinking
- The ability to act as a brokers and knowledge managers for available knowledge in the community, globally and through communities of practice
- An understanding of the critical role of emotional intelligence in the development of a commitment to learning
- Strong knowledge of a discipline (or subject) coupled with an ability to link this discipline to others
- A passion for creativity.

Also required is a high degree of accountability for learning and learning outcomes. By "accountability" here we do not mean managerial accountability (accountability to the system and its management) but to the student, the parent and the community as well as to their profession – what we might refer to as *professional accountability*. The teacher in this conception is accountable not just for outcomes, but for the design, process of learning and for connecting this learning to community expectations for the work of the school.

This conception of teaching is not new, but carries many implications, especially for teacher education and for ongoing professional development and the school. Let us look at these implications in the context of a human capital development framework for teachers – the EU Framework released in connection with *Education and Training 2010*[98], adopted by the Commission in 2004, taking into account the modifications of this document, especially the conclusions of the recent November 2009 Ministerial discussions concerning the professional development of teachers and school leaders.

The principles are clear. Teaching should be: (a) a well qualified profession; (b) located as a set of professional practices within the context of lifelong learning; (c) a profession that permits mobility between countries; and (d) a profession based on partnership with a range of stakeholders. Further, teaching and teacher education should be evidence based and strongly linked to a community of practice.

When the statement turns to competency, the Commission is vague. They emphasize the importance of a thoroughgoing knowledge of a discipline or subject, and then emphasize: (a) the ability to work with others so that they are able to nurture the skills and abilities of every learner and engage in social inclusion; (b) the ability of teachers to work with knowledge, technology and information - in particular, teachers need to be able to "build and maintain learning environments" and "retain the intellectual freedom to make choices and deliver education", making appropriate use of ICT as they support learners in social networks in which information can be found and built; and (c) the ability to work in society; they should be engaged in their community, participate in the tasks of enabling social and skills based mobility and enabling citizenship.

What they do not emphasize, but need to, is the importance of doing all of this in the context of a human capital strategy which emphasizes creativity, innovation, problem solving, and the skills required to enable each learner to develop in a way that enables them to be both actively engaged in designing and assessing their learning, and be able to develop their capacities. The November 2009 discussion of teacher education by European Ministers of Education, however, does move in this direction, and emphasizes the need for specific supports for teachers at all stages of their development, most especially in the early years following their entry into the profession. They will need this support if they are to display the competencies related to the creativity and innovation strategy outlined here.

Governments who have pursued certain strategies, such as the factory strategy of batch processing and quality inspection described above have generally indicated a lack of trust in teaching as a profession capable of enabling learning without strong and centralized 'command and control' curriculum guidance, targets and rigorous accountability measures. Indeed, some have suggested that these strategies have de-professionalized teaching, limiting the scope of professional discretion and control which teachers have over both what and how they engage learners in the task of learning. A key assumption of a focus on design and creativity as a strategy for education is that teaching, as a profession, needs to be strengthened, supported and developed. In particular, an investment strategy for teacher education and professional development is needed. These investments need to focus on broadening the teachers' ability to work with others on wicked problems, strengthening their own design skills and creativity and enabling the teacher to see the classroom as a base for learning, not the only place where learning can take place.

The Outcomes of Teaching

Good teaching is assessed in a variety of ways. One is through the outcomes achieved by the student – the concrete results of formative and summative assessment. A second is the teachers' own assessment of the progress made by each learner in their care. But the critical assessment which the teacher and students each needs to focus on is student engagement; the best predictor of learning outcomes.

There are five levels of student engagement:

Intrinsically Engaged Learners
• Student sees the activity as personally meaningful.
• The student's level of interest is sufficiently high that he persists in the face of difficulty.
• The student finds the task sufficiently challenging that he believes he will accomplish something of worth by doing it.
• The student's emphasis is on optimum performance and on "getting it right."

Tactically Engaged Learners
• The official reason for the work is not the reason the student does the work; she substitutes her own goals for the goals of the work.
• The substituted goals are instrumental; grades, class rank, college acceptance, and parental approval.
• The focus is on what it takes to get the desired personal

outcome rather than on the nature of the task itself; satisfactions are extrinsic.

• If the task doesn't promise to meet the extrinsic goal, the student will abandon it.

Compliant Students

• The work has no meaning to the student and is not connected to what does have meaning.
• There are no substitute goals for the student.
• The student seeks to avoid either confrontation or approbation.
• The emphasis is on minimums and exit requirements: "What do I have to do to get this over with and get out?"

Withdrawn Students

• The student is disengaged from current classroom activities and goals. The student is thinking about other things or is emotionally withdrawn from the action.
• The student rejects both the official goals and the official means of achieving the goals.
• The student feels unable to do what is being asked, or is uncertain about what is being asked.

Defiant Students

• The student is disengaged from current classroom activities and goals.
• The student is actively engaged in another agenda.
• The student creates her own means and her own goals.
• The student's rebellion is usually seen in acting out, and often in encouraging others to rebel.

Teachers have explored teaching and classroom strategies which seek to increase the number of students in the first two categories while at the same time reducing the number in the last two. What is key to achieving this is not technology (though this can be of assistance), but the skills and abilities of the teacher and in particular their ability to forge both an emotional and intellectual connection to the learner. The work of teaching is about hearts and minds. It is about the teacher modelling engagement in the work of the class through their own commitment to design, critical thinking and developing a solution to a wicked problem – they are learners too.

The challenge for school systems is finding the 'hooks' and 'handles' that create a connection between learners, teachers and the work of learning. Some have referred to this as "authentic learning"; learning through applied work[99]. Others call this engagement. Engaging learners in their own learning while developing, explicitly or implicitly, the outcomes identified in the previous chapter is the work of the teacher.

The Challenge

This conception of teaching is different from that which many parents experienced. 'Chalk and talk' (or 'click, point and tell' for Smart Board® teachers) is what parents expect school to be like. They don't expect to find teachers engaged in design, dialectic or exploratory critical thinking. They expect textbooks, not knowledge quests. They expect formalism, not informality. Indeed, when this author began teaching in this new way a fellow (and unsympathetic) teacher burst into a high school class I was teaching with the intention of restoring order when he suddenly saw me in the midst of a group of highly engaged (and noisy) learners – "Sorry", he said, "I came in to quell a riot, I didn't realize you were trying to teach". The students laughed and then one teenage girl, normally shy and reserved, said "we're busy learning, sir, sorry if we were a little noisy, but we all just made a big discovery! It was great!" He was suitably diminished. He also apologized over a beer some days later.

And this is the final point of this chapter, and a real challenge for many teachers. Learning and teaching are supposed to be fun! While teachers engage in the hard work of basic design of problem based learning, the execution the design and the pursuit of the challenge is meant to be an enjoyable, humorous journey of discovery (even when teachers think they have been on the journey before). Make it fun – there's a challenge!

Chapter 5: Technology, Learning, Learners and the Teacher

Introduction

Most people, when asked to describe a computer, will describe a box for the 'hardware', a keyboard, monitor and a mouse. They do not describe their car as a computer aided device (although any car has several on board), or their Blackberry, SmartPhone phone, television, iPod,iPad, iPhone, Play Station or game device — all of which are digital devices. The GPS system, which aids navigation in a car or through a handheld device, is a digital device: a computer.

During the next twenty years, we will see new devices which permit many tasks to be undertaken with the support of digital technologies. For example, it will soon be possible for a voice activated message from a cell phone to be received by the nearest ATM machine which will then allocate funds to that cell phone which will be used as the basis of individual financial transactions with speech recognition and other bio-metric security systems. This will be accelerated by the decision of some countries to stop using cheques for banking.

Home entertainment systems can now be wirelessly connected to devices which will permit the off air recording of television and radio programs from around the world and the downloading of music, movies and other forms of network broadcast media — thus creating personalized media centres in the home — independent of the broadcast schedules of organizations like BBC, ITV, CBC, Sky and CNN. These can be wirelessly transferred to a car, a handheld device, cell phone or iPod and be viewed by that person, wherever he or she is. More people now watch movies from such systems than watch them on broadcast TV or at the cinema. The growth of *Netflix* has enabled this as has the developments in home entertainments technologies.

As voice recognition and activation becomes more dominant, and simultaneous digital translation more efficient (significant new devices are expected in 2012-15), new devices permitting individuals to interact with others who speak different languages will emerge so that simultaneous translation is possible. Google Translate now makes translation of documents from one language to another relatively easy[100].

Ray Kurzweil, a pioneer inventor, has developed a 'seeing eye' cell phone which can 'read' a page and provide a voice reading of the page, and will soon be offering translation. It can also now identify what someone is wearing, different currency notes and will soon have a range of functions – very powerful for the blind or partially sighted.[101]

Don't think of computers as boxes, keyboards, mice and screens; think of devices. Don't think of computers as being in a particular place, they are wherever we are. Don't think of devices as hand-held or lap top, think of them as biological implants, very small devices added to watches or spectacles or as part of one's clothing. All of these are available now. What will happen between now and 2025 is that they will be more widespread, more varied, less expensive and able to handle very complex processes.

In this chapter, the current and coming technologies which could have an impact on learning are reviewed and their implications discussed. The aim is to paint a picture of a very different future which our learners will understand faster than our school systems can respond. While some of the material in this chapter may appear to some readers to be very futuristic and far fetched, everything presented here is in development or testing at the time of writing. Just because you may not be aware of it, doesn't mean that it is not likely to occur.

Once we have described the technological developments, we will look at the implications for teaching and learning and suggest some challenges which need to be addressed. The aim is not to present a picture of technological inevitability, but to present a realistic (if futuristic) understanding of what technology could offer and then to look at what we need to be working on as teachers to enable a sensible and focused leveraging of technology in terms of the purposes of learning, as outlined in earlier chapters.

Some readers may find this chapter discomforting.

Key Technological Developments

The World Wide Web is currently a very big collection of randomly organized materials, some of which is helpful. It contains many accurate and helpful pieces of information, and a larger number of unhelpful, inaccurate and often misleading pieces of information. Given its open nature, anyone can post anything on the web at any time and, with current technology, few technical skills are needed to do so.

When we think of the web we think of search engines like Google, Yahoo and others. Without these, we would be unable to narrow our search of the materials available. But these are very inefficient ways of getting at the information and, depending on which search engine is used; they search the web in different ways with very different results.

Three things will change the way we experience the World Wide Web. These are: (a) software agents; (b) developments in machine and artificial intelligence; and (c) the semantic web.

Software Agents

Software agents are computer programs capable of acting autonomously and whose awareness of their environment and apparent goal-oriented behaviour make them seem intelligent. Many visions of the expanding role that computer technology will play in every aspect of life to 2025 implicitly assume there will be major breakthroughs in our ability to design, build, and manage intelligent software agents[102].

The steady growth in Internet usage and the movement of businesses to the web to connect with customers, suppliers, and partners have created an opportunity for agent technology to play an important role in automating processes, bringing intelligence to the network, autonomously carrying out mundane tasks, enriching application-to-application communication, and improving decision-making.

Implications of these Developments: The web will shift from being a 'minefield' of information to being a knowledge repository which continually updates and corrects itself and provides knowledge 'packets' (custom built, intelligent packages of knowledge) that users want to help with learning, understanding and decision-making. Rather than us searching the web, the web will be proactive and prompt us whenever new knowledge is available on topics it knows we have an interest in. It will therefore become more personalized.

Machine and Artificial Intelligence

To achieve its potential by 2025, software agent technologies must capture intelligence in software and use this intelligence to allow programs to reason like humans. To this end, software agents must rely on techniques in learning, reasoning, planning, problem solving, and related areas. This machine intelligence will provide the techniques and algorithms that are used to; model the environment in which an agent operates; define the agent's goals; and specify the plan and associated actions the agent undertakes to achieve its goal. In particular, contributions from several fields of artificial intelligence will be used in developing agent and agent-based systems:

- **Reasoning system** — In planning their actions and making decisions, agents require the ability to reason about what to do and when to do it, particularly for actions they have not been instructed specifically to perform, requiring algorithms and techniques for reasoning.
- **Natural language processing** — The capacity to interact with humans to receive tasks or directions or to relay

information in natural language — that is, using statements in a human language rather than requiring a specially defined command language with a rigid syntax — requires ongoing research to improve the accuracy and effectiveness of these systems.

- **Neural networks** — Information processing systems use a large number of highly interconnected processing elements that are analogous to neurons and are linked with weighted connections analogous to synapses. As a result, neural networks can be used for "on the fly" learning, particularly where it involves the identification and application of patterns. In August 2011, IBM announced that it had produced "chips" which could mimic the synaptic learning processes used by the human brain – chips that can learn and remember patterns. This new chip will accelerate the development of neural networks.
- **Machine learning** — Machine learning techniques are used to develop systems that are capable of acquiring knowledge and integrating it with what they already know, resulting in autonomous learning devices. Known as "cognitive computers", these devices (now in production) are currently being used for environmental monitoring (linked to networks of sensor devices) and for understanding human behaviour.

Implications of these Developments: The web will make increasing use of artificial intelligence to gather, package and refine knowledge related to user needs and will begin to anticipate these needs and automatically personalize them for the user. For example, a student known to be having difficulty understanding one concept will be able to access thirty examples of this concept in action linked to all of his or her past web searches. We will increasingly be able to use natural language (both text and voice) to interact with digital devices and this will enable us to build a different kind of relationship with the web — it will become a meaningful, personalized knowledge utility.

The Semantic Web

The majority of content on the web is meant to be read by humans, not by software. However, the web's capabilities would be augmented significantly if content were represented in such a way that software could understand it as well. Understanding, in this case, means recognizing the intended meaning of content on a collection of web pages — having a contextual or semantic understanding. Put simply: we need our web agents to be able to read, understand both the words and their intentions, and then provide a summary/analysis and interpretation of these resources to us.

Significant work is underway to permit such semantic use of web-based information resources — turning information into knowledge. For example, the British software product "Autonomy", purchased by Hewlett Packard in August 2011, permits a user to begin typing a document and the system will match the ideas (not the words) in the document to relevant materials either on that organization's own servers or the World Wide Web and make them available to the user, constantly adjusting them as the ideas the user is typing emerge[103].

Another example would be someone trying to understand three different interpretations of a historical event — the semantic web could offer a summary of the three different views, using all of the available materials on the web.

Implications of these Developments: Rather than listing over 10.7m documents on diabetes available on the web, the system will read them, summarize them and make recommendations about diabetes based on the user's natural language query. This provides a basis for the web to be an intelligent partner for all learning activities and may, especially at an instructional level, provide an opportunity for the web to replace some basic teaching.

Positional Learning (GPS Enabled Learning)

A number of companies are working on learning projects where learning is linked to location. As you walk through a location with a hand held device or cell phone connected to a wireless network the learning system provides information ("you are standing on the spot in which the oldest dinosaur on the world was found"), pose questions or provide knowledge relevant to learner needs. The information can be presented in the form of a game (e.g. "Lost") and will generally be highly interactive. A person walking through an old mine can learn about its history, be challenged about safety issues or specific incidents that happened in the mine or can interact with a range of characters using simulation.

There is no reason that such a set of learning objects, tools and resources could not be deployed initially for key locations for learning and then everywhere in the world. It would be invaluable for safety education ("six feet in front of you is a red handle — do not touch this, it opens a door to an area you are not certified to enter") and other forms of learning.

It will soon be possible to walk in downtown Toronto or London or Cairo and ask "where is the nearest Banking Machine?" and your cell phone will give directions. It is a small step to make this proactive rather than reactive. As systems gain the ability to understand thought patterns, the knowledge hub can respond ("I hear you thinking about Indian food, there is a highly-rated Indian restaurant two blocks east from here…" or "remember two weeks ago you were wondering what an isosceles triangle was, if you look at the design of the office building in front of you and to your left, you will see six of them — want me to show you?").

Implications of these Developments: Learning linked to location will be a fast growing phenomenon in 2012 and beyond. As more devices begin to have 3D facilities and more opportunities to connect to local content, learning 'layers' will emerge where the learner can chose what topics (layers) they wish to experience in which locations. They will be able to 'rehearse' their experience in simulators before getting there. One obvious application is in an art gallery or museum, extending the current audio tour into location-specific audio-visual tours where the artist can speak about the painting you are looking at or respond to questions you may ask (simulated). But other locations may be in food stores where you can ask how to prepare a particular vegetable or meal, and your cell phone will show you.

Simulation

Simulation technologies are in widespread use, including in use by many of Northern Ontario's colleges and universities. They are used by military organizations to simulate battle conditions, air assault and specific maneuvers. They are used by planners to simulate traffic and driving conditions, and are at the heart of computer games. They are used in teaching to simulate managerial challenges, medical conditions, engineering or mathematical problems.

Simulations are becoming more powerful and effective. Building on gaming technologies and artificial intelligence, an individual can now experience a range of simulated environments in which they can practice and demonstrate skills and competencies safely. For example, doctors can practice surgery using the MRI images of their patient before the patient comes in for surgery, and forecast and simulate the consequences of that surgery[104]. A student learning how to assemble a turbine can do so in a simulated environment and test the simulated turbine under a range of conditions, all in the safety of a three dimensional laboratory, using super fast computers.

As three dimensional visualization (virtual reality) becomes more available and more commonly used, emerging technologies, such as highly interactive and immersive virtual reality will become an important part of many learning and work processes. Virtual reality simulations will provide unparalleled power to explore ideas and experiences and to communicate what we learn in very new ways. A student will be able to practice all of the skills of, say, a registered nursing program or an electrical engineering degree in a virtual simulation environment before being able to practice on human subjects or in a construction project. A historian will be able to recreate historical events and students will be able to interact with the characters in these events.

By 2025 it will be possible to undertake a wide range of simulated activities and look at a range of different outcomes (if I had chosen X, then…instead of what actually happened when I chose Y…). For example, new product testing (including drug testing) will involve simulation, looking at the impact a drug will have on a range of different conditions in simulated 'people' with different symptoms. Many skills-based simulations will be available – we'll ask, "want to know how to change an engine in a car?" – then go to the simulator and practice. The quality of the learning experience (it will be an experience, not just a lecture or an account in a text) will be enriched.

Implications of these Developments: There are several: (a) trades education could be significantly improved and the time taken to secure a "ticket" reduced by the effective use of complex simulations; (b) professional education could be enhanced by real time simulation (simulators for dentists, doctors, psychologists, nurses, teachers, lawyers, accountants, fire fighters and many others); and (c) continued education for professionals (skills updating) can be enhanced and made available 24/7 through simulations of increasing complexity. Simulations can be shared within and across jurisdictions — Ontario could specialize in some medical conditions, Québec in others and engage in exchange arrangements so as to quickly make available simulations to improve medical education. Simulation will become an expectation of students, especially those just born who will play 3D games and become used to holographic gaming in 2020 and beyond.

Social Networks

Critical developments have also taken place in how social networks function on the web. In the very important text *No Size Fits All*[105], Tom Hayes and Michael Malone document the way in which ideas, learning and opportunities for deepening understanding and sharing information are now increasingly occurring through such media as Facebook, MySpace, LinkedIn and Ning. LinkedIn, for example, is a professional networking version of Facebook. It currently has some 100 million users and users create groups, many of which can be seen as dedicated learning groups. Facebook has, at the time of writing, over 650 million users, 75% of whom post daily. Posting a problem or challenge can result in several helpful connections and suggestions in just a few hours. President Obama owes his election as President of the United States in part to his team's ability to leverage social networks to promote ideas, counter rumours and encourage networking.

Some uses of social networks, such as Twitter, are inane. People post what colour socks they are wearing. But other uses are profound. The overthrow of the regime in Egypt was organized through a combination of Facebook and Twitter, with help from YouTube. People trapped in buildings after the Japanese earthquake and tsunami were found by a combination of GPS technology embedded in SmartPhones and Twitter. Musicians can now become instant hits by posting music videos on YouTube – which is how Simon Cowell found a fourteen year old singer and contracted her for a $1million contract.

Teachers often see social networking – Facebook, MySpace, Twitter – as a means of distraction, and they are right to do so. But the educational value of these networks is being lost in many schools by outright bans and Smartphone lock-downs. Rather than banning these networks, schools need to leverage them for problem solving, cross-cultural sharing and as knowledge hubs. One growing use of these networks is for precisely these purposes.

Implications of these Developments: Social networks are here to stay and learners will use them effectively for a variety of purposes. They need support in using these resources "smartly" – lean social networking is a concept whose time has come. But teachers should be setting knowledge challenges and inspiring students to leverage their networks for learning. Challenging a group of learners to use their networks to understand a problem, to collect data or to share ideas is a more constructive response to the ubiquity of these networks than banning access to them. When they are being used as a distraction, the question to ask is not "how do I stop this?", but "how can I engage this person or group of people in using these social networks for an engaging learning challenge?"

Robots

Robots are extensively used in manufacturing systems (especially automotive manufacturing) and are rapidly developing, especially as machine intelligence continues to develop and new substances solve mechanical problems in the durability and flexibility of robots as machines. We have a "science fiction view of robotics" based on a number of different movies, but the actual elements of the next stage of robotic development are gradually appearing. These are:

- Machine intelligence machines that can use natural language to access the semantic web, package information into intelligent forms and use this knowledge to shape the robot's behaviour.
- The ability of machines to 'see' – take visual images, process them, 'understand' (interpret) them and then act accordingly – is rapidly developing, especially in medical robots now being used to perform surgery.
- The growing use of touch sensitive systems enables robots to sense sensitivity, durability, plasticity and other properties of the things they touch. In keyhole surgery using robotics, this feature is of growing significance in the surgical removal of cancerous tumours, for example.
- The ability of machines to use logic and reasoning engines to make decisions.
- The ability of machines to patiently learn from its iterations of an activity or group of activities.

Robots are becoming sophisticated devices and are being used extensively in health care for a variety of purposes from surgical procedures, distribution of pharmaceutical products to hospital patients, intelligent analysis of diagnostic information (including MRI's, X Rays and medical tests) and after care for patients. In Japan, robots are used extensively in eldercare for counselling and support.

At the University of Wales, Mike Young has built and is using a scientific robot that can originate a hypothesis to explain a set of observations, carry out experiments in a laboratory, undertake measurements, analyze and interpret results. The system is able to improve its performance by learning from its experiences and by pulling information from the web. The robot has designed a range of experiments which, apart from being completed faster than a 'rival' human scientist, were also a third less expensive.

By 2015, the first machines that can see, hear, move and manipulate objects at a level roughly equivalent to human beings will have made their way from research labs into the marketplace[106]. These robots could well be able to 'think' as creatively as some human beings. Humanoid robots will cost less than the average car, and prices will continuously fall. A typical model will have two functioning arms, two legs and the normal human-type sensors like vision, hearing and touch. Power will be provided from small, easily recharged fuel cells. Equipped with powerful devices, the robot will gradually replace many 'people' functions in many organizations; checkouts in supermarkets; banking activities; forestry; construction; mining; hotel and restaurant services; financial advising; teacher aids in schools; coaching for some sports. Some airlines are looking at robotic pilots (as already used by some military forces) as a way of lowering costs and improving reliability. Many trains, such as the high speed rail link between the Vancouver airport and downtown Vancouver, are 'driverless'.

By 2025, some of the functions currently performed by people in schools, universities and colleges could be performed by robots; advising; financial services and administrative functions; teaching of basic skills and competencies; assignment marking (and not just for multiple choice assignments); and supporting students as coaches, guides and mentors.

Implications of these Developments: Robots will have a major impact on social and economic activity sometime after 2015¬2020. Some predict they will gradually find their way into many areas of life, whether they are physical robots (doing manual labour, repetitive tasks, intelligent tasks which require complex knowledge) or non-physical robots, like agents or learning networks. For education, key roles in administration could be undertaken by robots (advising, financial services, registry) and gradually more demanding functions requiring a high level of intelligence (instruction, coaching, assessing) could be undertaken by people-friendly robots. They are coming. The issue is how we wish to use them. One other implication: quality. By setting standards for all instruction through robots and by training robots to be thorough, we can ensure that standards are applied and maintained

The Human-Technology Interface

At some point (2025-2030), the power of the semantic web will exceed the power of a small human team working on a problem [107] . In part, this will be because we are using nanotechnology to speed the power of computational work and in part it will be because some simple computers will be so readily available everywhere that it will become natural to engage the power of the knowledge driven web to support human activity. We will be able to use these resources to support decision making, learning and well-being. A few examples:

- Human memory is equivalent to around 1013 "bits" of memory — for example, Shakespeare used 29,000 words to create some 100,000 meanings which is equivalent to around 1013 bits. By around 2018, we will be able to buy carbon memory tubes able to store this amount of memory (equivalent to a person's lifetime memory) for around $1,000. By around 2020, we will be able to create devices that can replicate the functioning of the human brain (using reverse engineering) for about $1,000. By around 2050 or sooner, this same $1,000 will buy the equivalent of the computing power of all of the people on earth[108].

- When coupled with machine and artificial intelligence and instant access to the semantic web through very fast, global wireless networks – new devices will support such things as thought driven access to information (you think – "what film was Denzel Washington in recently?" and the list appears on a hand held device, culled from the web and delivered by an intelligent agent which you have trained. Translation between languages will become ubiquitous, through either devices or implants (or combinations of both)[109].

Most people, on reading these descriptions, think "science fiction". All of these systems are in development at this time — thought based computing, nano-bots, intelligent implants, etc. – are in being explored for a variety of applications at the time of writing.

It is not being suggested here that technology will replace human interaction. Rather it is saying that a new set of interactions between technology and a person will be possible. As we start to replace damaged tissues, damaged neurological functions with digital devices and nano technologies, we will make breakthroughs which will change the relationship between knowledge, technology and biological persons.

Implications of these Developments: Knowledge (as opposed to just information) will be accessible in a usable form anytime, anywhere and be able to be accessed directly by the thought based intelligent devices (combinations of glasses and headphones linked to a wireless jacket receiver or hat).

Knowledge will be packaged by intelligent agents, working to meet the needs of their user. If the user has a clear need for knowledge (e.g. to master a given set of competencies), then agents will work out how best to deliver these. At some time in the future (probably mid to late century) we will have mechanisms to upload and download knowledge and skills to and from the brain directly — at this point, skills and ideas can be transferred quickly from one person to another or from one group to another.

Many see these developments as "scary", but they are being worked on now.

Users of Devices

Students beginning school next September will retire from the workforce between 2070 and 2080, if they enter it at all. Unlike their great grandfathers, most will occupy some 15-20 jobs in their work-life and stay no more than five to seven years with a single employer. Work-life balance for many of this iGen (also known as the "text generation" or Generation Z) will be a bigger issue than pensions. They will expect their employer to practice strategically focused human resource policies which aid their personal and professional development and will look to work as one source of satisfaction, but work will not be the focus for their life. They will bring to their work remarkable technical skills, a strong entrepreneurial outlook, a deep-seated social consciousness (especially with respect to the environment), and, like every new generation, a healthy dose of questioning and a desire for change.

As the costs of digital devices fall, access to education will be less about teacher:student ratios as it will be about bandwidth, networks of peer support and the capacity for adult coaching and learning outcomes and process assessment. Since these resources are global resources, the existing learning system paradigm will gradually be replaced through the choices made by learners acting as consumers of the knowledge products and services available on the web. These changes may look something like those featured in the following table.

FEATURE	OLD PARADIGM	NEW PARADIGM
Learning Unit	The Class	The Individual
Information	Lectures and Textbooks	Semantic Web
Knowledge	Seminars, Classes, Professors working with groups of students	Semantic Web, Simulation and Nanobot Technologies
Learner Support	Teachers, Teaching Assistants, Parents, Peers and Other Adults	Teachers, Other Adults, Global Peer Networks, Certified Assessors, Robots
Learner Assessment	Assignments, Lab Work	Simulations, Peer to Peer Competency Assessment, Teachers as Certified Assessors, Robots
Speed of Completion of a Program	Institutionally Determined	Individually Determined
Accreditation/Certification	Local	National, Multinational (e.g. NAFTA) and Global

Figure 7: From One Learning Systems Paradigm to Another

Students will leverage technology, peer networks, robots and artificial intelligence in support of their learning challenges before institutions adopt them — acting as consumers, they will drive some changes in the system. They will access knowledge from global knowledge engines available through the semantic web. They will seek credit recognition for their work. They will demand acknowledgement of learning from a variety of sources. The opportunity thus exists to shift to a new paradigm for the management of learning outcomes — a paradigm likely to be resisted by those committed to the old paradigm, which has a strong and successful six hundred year history.

The Implications for Teaching and Learning[110]

The implications of the foregoing review of technology developments, current and planned, are that teachers will not generally be required to provide the bulk of information or knowledge to a learner — many learners will be able to access such resources themselves. So what are teachers for?[111]

The literature on technology in education for the future suggests that, by around 2020, teachers in school will have the following primary tasks:

1. The design of authentic learning tasks[112] – meaningful challenges which require a student to master a body of knowledge and skills, either alone or in a group.
2. Being a mentor, coach and guide for a learner and their learning tasks — rather than being an 'instructor', the task of the professor or teacher will be to connect learning to the person; to make the learning personal and to support

learners who are struggling with their mastery of a skill, competency or challenge.

3. Developing a competency map for these tasks and integrating these maps into an accredited competency based program for assessment (formative and summative) and for feedback. This program may be a high school diploma, International Baccalaureate, a trades certification or part of a professional designation or other internationally accredited program.

4. Providing a systematic rubric for individual student assessment and feedback on their development in terms of the intended learning outcomes for their stage of development and education.

5. Engaging in professional development to keep their own knowledge and skills focused, current and effective.

The design of authentic tasks does not mean that the teacher supervises every step of the process a learner or group of learners uses to master the task — they may choose to do so or may choose to be a coach or mentor to the process. What is key is that the teacher becomes a coach to the learner and makes the learning experiences meaningful to the student or group of students.

Fundamentally, their instructional work will be largely replaced by their work in framing learning challenges and creating a process by which a student's competency can be assessed. They will also provide support for a learner to make intelligent choices as to where to look for appropriate learning opportunities from a global network of providers. They will coach, guide, assess and mentor rather than be the primary providers of instruction.

That is what the futuristic literature suggests. Current attempts to "get there" do not paint this same picture. We now explore several reasons why this proposed future is problematic.

The Digital Divide

The digital divide that separates people who have ready access to and a facility with technology from those who have limited or no access to technology and few skills is real and apparent in today's classrooms. Which side of the digital divide a person inhabits tends to be determined by the following factors[113]:

1. *Available Infrastructure*: With the exception of the school or public library, some communities do not have access to broadband services. Furthermore, some people have no secure place (other than an education centre or library) in which they can access technology for learning.
2. *Geography*: Rural students, especially those living on reserve or in remote communities, have less access to technology than their urban counterparts.
3. *Gender*: Females appear to be less interested in or have less access to the Internet and other technologies than males [114]
4. *Socioeconomic status*: Internet access and use as well as access to other technologies is a function of income, social class and employment status.
5. *Race*: Aboriginal students, especially those on reserve, are less likely to have access to technology than their non-Aboriginal counterparts.

Schools have to cope with students who range from being highly competent to nearly computer illiterate. To be used in a transformative way, technology must take these differences into account, recognizing that a student's ability to access and use technology is often related to his or her socioeconomic status.

While technology is a convenience for most students, for those with disabilities and special needs it can transform the learning experience. Assistive technologies, which are constantly improving, range from audio books and worksheets to optical character readers to speech-recognition programs to self-programming intelligent devices to advanced writing tablets (operable by a single finger or toe and—soon—by brain waves) to robotic assistants.

A protocol governing the development and design of these assistive technologies has emerged. Known as Universal Design for Learning (UDL) [115], the protocol stipulates that as new curricular materials and learning technologies are developed, they should be designed *from the beginning* to be flexible enough to accommodate the unique learning styles of a wide range of people, including students with disabilities. UDL ensures, for example, that web pages are accessible to people with disabilities, that textbooks and other curricular materials are published both electronically and in paper, that videos are captioned or narrated, that word processors are capable of predicting the word that someone is trying to enter, that spell checkers and dialog boxes can 'speak', that programs have voice-recognition capabilities and that menus include pictures. UDL does not eliminate the need for assistive technology; students with disabilities will continue to need communication aids, visual aids, wheelchairs and adapted toys in order to interact more fully with their environment. However, building accessibility into new technologies and curricular materials *as they are developed* helps to ensure that children with disabilities will be able to take advantage of most of the learning opportunities that are available to the general student population.

How will pedagogical practices and the curriculum need to change to accommodate the digital generation and those with differing levels of access to these technologies; from none through some to ubiquity? Is engaging them and meeting their immediate needs *all* that matters, or are educators also responsible for meeting their long-term psycho-social and economic needs? What about the needs of the wider community? Which aspects of so-called traditional education should be preserved and which should be abandoned? On what basis should these decisions be made?

Transformation of Schools and Technology

There are a variety of reasons for the current relatively low level of technology use in schools in comparison with other sectors of the economy – health, banking, travel, and music for instance. Here are a few:

1. *Most schools are not organized in a way that supports transformative changes.* As a result, any changes that are made tend to be gradual, incremental and hesitant. All the partners—parents, teachers, administrators, students and the community—may resist transformative change, often for good reasons. One reason is the education policy makers are constantly proposing radical reforms to the school system. If educators were to act on each proposed reform, the ministry of education would likely regard them as perennially failing institutions. Although the

inherent conservatism of educational systems helps protect schools from pointless change, it also renders them quite resistant to beneficial innovations. For schools to embrace sustainable change, they need compelling evidence, the necessary resources and a substantial investment in professional development.

2. *Teachers do not always have the skills necessary to use technology as a tool for transforming learning.* Although a growing number of teachers have become quite adept at using technology, the majority still find technology a challenge and, as a result, tend to rely on more conventional teaching tools. Even when jurisdictions invest in very basic technologies, such as SmartBoards™, teachers are relatively slow to adopt the newer methods. A major reason for the slow acceptance is the paucity of professional development opportunities for teachers. In one leading Canadian jurisdiction, schools have committed only between 2 and 3 per cent of their operating budgets to professional development since 1999, far below the 5 to 10 per cent that other sectors spend on staff training[116].

3. *The ability of students to access and use technology varies considerably.* Although more of today's students have technical skills than was the case in the preceding generation, the digital divide still poses a major barrier to the widespread adoption of technology as a way of transforming the learning process. Aboriginal students living on reserves are particularly disadvantaged in this regard.

4. *Governments and school boards generally focus their technology spending on basic infrastructure rather than on transformative initiatives.* In other words, they tend to focus on the

technology itself (whether videoconferencing, SmartBoards™ or one-to-one wireless learning) rather than on how the technology can transform the learning process. Examples of transformative strategies including; teaching less and encouraging students to learn by undertaking projects; and doing away with textbooks and replacing the entire curriculum (math, science, social studies and language arts) for a particular grade with a set of technology-enabled activities designed to ensure the same learning outcomes. Rather than having a technology branch, school systems should create an "innovation branch," the purpose of which would be to develop the curriculum in a way that increases student engagement and improves learning outcomes.

5. *Teachers are only moderately confident in their ability to incorporate technology into the teaching–learning* process. Even though the Internet has been around since 1994, school districts and many teachers are still clearly 'feeling their way' with respect to using technology to engage students and enhance learning. Indeed, some school districts now deny students access to such social networking media as Facebook and MySpace during class time. Others do not permit students to use mobile devices during class, even though many of these devices are now so sophisticated that they could serve as mobile learning centres, replete with access to the Internet, special applications, and audio and video materials.

6. *The national, State or Provincial curriculum specifies so many learning outcomes that teachers tend to rely on time-tested processes rather than risk using new technology-based approaches that might lower student scores on provincial achievement tests.* While acknowledging the potential

benefits of technology, many teachers do not feel that they have the time or the resources to make the transition from traditional methods of teaching to those that involve a greater reliance on technology.

7. *Teachers who risk using technology to transform their teaching practice receive little recognition.* In many school districts, being innovative in the classroom is seldom rewarded either by professional advancement or by peer recognition. Hargreaves and Shirley (2009) point out that many jurisdictions are addicted to undertaking initiatives that, while producing short-term improvements, fail to address the systemic issues that hinder teachers from embracing truly innovative practices. [117] In such jurisdictions, teachers are made to focus all their energy on complying with externally imposed mandates—with making what might be called "data-informed improvements"—rather than on exploring ways of transforming the teaching–learning process. "When schools follow policy mandates and pursue the relentless quest for short-term gains, they evolve into…addictive organizations".[118]

8. *Many schools exhibit a culture of compliance that inhibits innovation.* School administrators face a myriad of challenges: complying with accountability requirements imposed by the jurisdiction, dealing with an increasingly complex curriculum, supporting teachers whose technology skills may be limited and appeasing parents who may be resistant to change. As a result, their attempts to improve student learning are seldom more than moderately successful. Some projects carried out by the Alberta Initiative for School Improvement (AISI) and the Galileo Educational Network in Alberta, though modest in

scale, demonstrate what is possible. A review of AISI projects undertaken between 2003 and 2006 revealed that the projects that had the biggest impact (albeit a modest one) on student achievement and on teacher, student and parent satisfaction were those involving technology [119]. As Hargreaves and Fink (2006) observe, "change in education is easy to propose, hard to implement, and extraordinarily difficult to sustain."[120]

Although striving to improve schools on a continuous basis is not necessarily a bad thing, such an approach is not the hallmark of progressive organizations. A much more productive approach is to initiate a cycle of transformation, consolidate the gains achieved and then start a new cycle of transformation. Although change is disruptive, such a cyclical approach leads to higher productivity, improved outcomes and higher levels of employee and 'customer' satisfaction over time[121].

The Agenda for Teachers and Technology

In 2007, the Canadian Council on Learning (CCL) and the Canadian Educational Association (CEA) embarked on a multi-year initiative to transform the environment in which students learn [122]. Their efforts at transformation were based on the following principles:

1. *Teachers are designers of learning.* Rather than teaching to the test, teaching the textbook, or delivering the provincial curriculum as written, teachers use their training, their

professional experience and their participation in communities of practice to design meaningful learning experiences tailored to meet the unique needs of their students. Teachers understand that the community has entrusted them with the task of designing meaningful and memorable learning activities that help students improve their skills, knowledge and understanding.

2. *The work that students are asked to undertake is worth their time and attention.* The learning that students engage in is personally meaningful, intellectually challenging and capable of sustaining their interest over time. In other words, the learning tasks are authentic and are intended for an authentic audience.

3. *Assessment practices improve student learning and guide teaching.* Students and teachers work together to create assessment criteria. They also undertake continuous assessment activities designed not only to improve learning but also to foster student engagement and collaboration. Students also help to assess their peers; a skill that they will need in the 21st century workplace[123].

4. *Teachers encourage students to develop a variety of interdependent relationships.* Teachers encourage students to connect with other students; to participate in communities of interest, and to access (both in person and online) local, regional and global sources of knowledge related to the subjects they are studying. Such connections foster collaboration, cooperation, engagement and the development of social skills [124]. Teachers should also participate in peer networks at the local, regional and global level.

5. *Teachers improve their practice in the company of their peers.*
    Working closely with their peers on an ongoing basis
    helps teachers to become more effective and innovative in
    their teaching practice. In addition to constituting a
    professional development opportunity, participating in a
    community of practice is an integral part of transforming
    the teaching/learning process in a way that improves
    student learning.

These principles, if followed, are the key to transforming schools
in a way that will enable them to adequately prepare students to
function in the knowledge economy of the 21st century. Teachers
working in such schools will clearly need not only access to
technology but facility in integrating that technology seamlessly
into their teaching practice. They need support, investment and
professional development to do so. But they should be driving
these developments – as professionals.

The Challenge

In this rather long, but important chapter, several aspects of the future development of technology are reviewed and the implications of these developments for the process of learning, teaching and knowledge explorations are discussed. Several major issues are raised throughout the chapter which will be discomforting to many teachers and educational administrators.

The fundamental challenge being explored here is deceptively simple: how do we leverage current and emerging technology to increase the quality, depth and meaning of adult:student interactions in education? How can we increase student engagement with learning, knowledge and understanding so as to encourage their passion for learning?

It is a major challenge, and one we had better get used to addressing as technology is progressing faster than our ability to answer this question.

Chapter 6: Personalized Learning

Introduction

Another key idea which is informing thinking about the future of schools, teaching and learning is the construct of 'personalizing learning'. In part driven by the emergence of technologies just described, but also by an ideological commitment to a different model of public services, the ideology of 'personalizing' learning is seductive. It implies that, through differentiated instruction and personalized programs for learning, we can increase learner engagement and improve learning outcomes. But what does personalized learning actually mean?

It could and does mean a variety of different things to different people. During the last year, the author has observed nine very different versions of 'personalized learning' from conferences, workshops and publications. They are: *Needs + Wants*

1. **Curriculum designed uniquely for each learner** – this is more likely customized learning, based on an assessment of the learners' needs, learning style and capacities. While some special needs students may experience this form of instruction, it is not at all likely to be widespread and available to all in a public education system due to cost constraints, the batch processing model of learning in common use and the current skill level, constraints and experience of teachers.

2. **A personal route through curriculum choices linked to interests, career planning and skills** – using course

choice to find a pathway to an education which reflects the person making these choices. This was very much the core of the innovation in Finnish high schools around a decade ago and is now being replicated in other systems.

3. **1:1 instruction** – ensuring that each learner receives personal instruction for each subject they require instruction in; again, unlikely in a public education system due to cost and related constraints, except in special circumstances.

4. **Online learning**– anytime, anywhere: this is e-learning and not necessarily personalized. Some school systems are seeing this as a way of personalizing education, especially when the learner can start any course at anytime and complete the exam/assessment whenever they are ready to do so.

5. **Work based learning credits + credits from completion of school or non-school courses** - permitting those high school students who also work to receive credit for work-based learning while also earning credits for their school work – connecting learning to the personal choices of individuals.

6. **Challenge based learning credits** – where the learner, at a point of their choosing, challenges a course in terms of assessment and credit once they have learned what they need to be successful.

7. **Changing the pacing of learning** – enabling some learners to 'fast track' and some to go at a slower pace – calling an assessment at any time.

8. **Learning linked to learning styles** – learning is linked to different learning styles and the same objectives are

achieved through a variety of learning routes (a form of differentiated instruction).

9. **Differential supports for learning** – almost all "credited" learning (learning for credit) is currently done by teachers, but there are others in the community with significant knowledge and skill who could make learning possible. Musicians, artists, artisans, craftspeople, culinary artists (cooks, chefs) and many more. Why not permit them to offer instruction which is recognized in the learner's profile?

This is confusing. We need to understand more about this construct: where it came from and where it is headed.

Where did Personalized Learning Come From?

The following quotation from Pearson, the educational publisher, makes clear that there is an agenda behind their push to leverage technology to personalize learning:

still stuck on industry model.

> Rapid advances taking place in technological development must be integrally connected to our education system if U.S. students are to continue to compete successfully on the world stage, and a vital part of that transformation must be the personalizing of instructional delivery. As a U.S. Dept. of Education position paper cited in Personalized Learning notes, "We have seen our world change around us and now need to retool our education system to respond."

"Education does not work through a 'one-size-fits-all' model," said Will Ethridge, CEO of Pearson's North

American education businesses. "Students have different learning styles, needs, and priorities, and there is an increasing demand for technologies that personalize the learning experience. Our challenge is to continue to create the tools that ensure relevance and success for 21st Century learners, as well as to deliver cost and instructional efficiencies to institutions."

Research makes clear that personalized learning, combined with the power of technology, greatly improves and accelerates student success rates. Over the past decade, the National Center for Academic Transformation's post-secondary course redesign program has proven that through more effective use of information and technology, it is possible to produce better learning outcomes at reduced cost. NCAT's Program in Course Redesign resulted in 25 of the 30 course redesign projects showing significant increase in student learning, with all 30 projects reducing their costs by an average of 37 percent - a collective annual savings of approximately $3 million[125]."

So one origin of personalized learning is the idea that, harnessing the power of technology, school jurisdictions can reduce the costs of education by leveraging online learning. While this quotation focuses on postsecondary education (college and university programming), Pearson is also engaged in the same work at the level of the school.

In this context, it is useful to remember that e-learning is an industry category, that the industry is currently (2011) worth some $56.8billion worldwide, and that it is growing at a compound annual growth rate (CAGR) of 12.5%. It is anticipated to be a $100 billion industry by 2018 or sooner[126]. Pearson is vying to be a major player in this industry sector.

A second starting point for personalized learning is a political agenda[127]. Historically, the term personalized learning was first used in a 2003 speech by the Honourable David Miliband, then-minister of state for School Standards for England and Wales, who pronounced that "personalised learning demands that every aspect of teaching and support is designed around a pupil's needs" (quoted in David Hargreaves, 2004)[128]. This speech was driven by the Blair government's desire to reorganize the way services were delivered, moving from the universal provision of services by government (batched services that recipients were fitted into) toward a more personalized approach that was hinged on each citizen's individual choices and actions, based on a 'menu' of available public services, supports and tax credits.

Thus personalized learning became bound up in a larger framework of the customization of public services. In the healthcare, social service and education sectors, the appeal was to the consumer side of a citizenry looking for a promise of choice, greater flexibility and efficiencies for the individual. David Cameron, Britain's latest Prime Minister, is taking this further and permitting personalized social service (including education, child care, and mental health) to be delivered locally by *any* competent organization – public or private, with an agreed rate of payment paid for from the public purse.

David Hargreaves has been instrumental in defining the idea by establishing a range of actions or gateways to personalizing learning[129]. Andy Hargreaves and Dennis Shirley (2009)[130] have provided a critical assessment of this approach as being a new way to manage and market education and learning. In their book *The Fourth Way*, Hargreaves and Shirley make this statement:

> ...[David Hargreaves] initially referred to personalization in terms of its synonym, "customization" in the business world. With customized learning, students access existing and *unchanged kinds of conventional learning* through different means—on site or off site, online or offline, in school or out of school, quickly or slowly. . . . *But the nature of learning is not transformed into something deeper, more challenging, and more connected to compelling issues in their world and their lives.* Twenty first century schools must also embrace deeper virtues and values such as courage, compassion, service, sacrifice, long-term commitment and perseverance. Customized learning is pleasurable and instantly gratifying. Nevertheless it ultimately becomes just one more process of business-driven training delivered to satisfy individual consumer tastes and desires. (p. 84 – my emphasis)

- suggesting that personalized learning is a form of instant download of learning opportunities awaiting 'consumption'.

For others, personalized learning appears to mean a combination of some or all of these key ideas:

- students progress in programs at a pace that suits their needs and enhances their success.
- students build on individual strengths and achievements, pursue their passions and interests, and learn in ways that are consistent with their individual learning styles.

- barriers to learning are reduced to allow more flexible hours of instruction and schedules.
- students have access to a greater variety of learning experiences that include and extend beyond traditional education settings and benefit from increased community involvement in their learning.
- multi-disciplinary learning teams comprising teachers, teacher assistants, health professionals, social workers, community members, and parents provide 'wrap-around' supports and services to optimize student success.
- students contribute to diverse learning communities in which the social component of learning and the development and sharing of knowledge is central to their educational experience.
- technology and community-based activities are used to enrich learning experiences and enable students to apply their learning in real-life contexts.
- there is a greater emphasis on assessment for learning (i.e., an ongoing exchange of information between students and teachers about student progress toward clearly specified learner outcomes).
- students are lifelong learners who thrive in, and adapt to, a complex and rapidly changing world.

To make matters more complicated, personalized learning and differentiated instruction have in some writing become synonymous, even though the historiographies and semiotics of this language are very different indeed. One has its roots in politics and business ("personalization") and the other its roots in the classroom practices of teachers ("differentiated instruction"), as Michael Fullan has observed[131].

Nonetheless, the combination of technology, problem based learning, open classroom technologies and the blurring of the boundaries between school and home make personalized learning a possibility.

What Personalized Learning Should Mean

Putting aside the starting points for personalized learning, what could this mean for a rethink of our schools and the processes of teaching and learning? When several of us looked at this when preparing for a symposium for teachers and administrators from Finland and Alberta, we suggested[132] that personalized learning could mean some or all of these things:

1. Personalized learning means learning which is meaningful and mindful for the learner. Rather than increasing the ways in which the same education is delivered – repackaging (which can be an important feature, as we shall see) – the real challenge is to make the learning activities in which the student is engaged meaningful to the learner in both intellectual and emotional terms. Hence the emphasis earlier in this book on "wicked problems" which challenge the hearts and minds of learners (see Chapter 3), and a focus on facilitative and mindful teaching (Chapter 4).

2. Personalized learning means more choices for students – more routes to a high school diploma or matriculation. Rather than 'one size fits all', several different high school diplomas are made available and students choose their pathways to these diplomas in terms of small credit units which they accumulate. Some credits are acceptable across all of the available diplomas, while others can only be

used for some. Student choice of their route through school personalizes their learning.

3. Personalized learning means more opportunities to pace when study occurs and when assessment occurs – students can call assessment when they are ready to do so (learning is no longer linked to 'time served in the classroom' but to outcomes). The most underused resource in school systems is time. By batch processing students and having limited set dates for examinations (two dates a year for diploma exams in many jurisdictions) students are constrained. If such assessment points were available every day, anytime, students could fast track some assessments and slow others down, thus enabling them to self pace. By having weekly start dates for every credit activity in school, students could also start when they want, thus enabling a more personalized management of their curriculum. While these steps seem radical, most alternative school programs currently practice versions of these policies.

4. Personalized learning requires a significant investment in advising and guidance. Many students make choices based on poor or limited information. To truly personalize a learning system, students need the best possible guidance and information both about what is involved in a learning choice (time, knowledge, skill, capacities) and about the consequences of their choices for their subsequent learning and work careers.

5. Learners can gain credit towards their schooling from a variety of sources – e.g. International Baccalaureate, company based training, college or university credit, music certification programs (e.g. Royal Academy of Music). The school has several functions, a key one being

the recognition of learning for credit. If schools moved away from long courses with standard examinations and towards more short courses with smaller credit rating, then a great deal of learning activities undertaken outside of the school could be recognized for credit. For example, a student who works as a line cook part time while attending high school could obtain some culinary arts credits. In this way, the student begins to understand the connection between learning and work but also can personalize their learning portfolio through the choices they make of what to submit for credit assessment.

6. Students collaborate and have a voice in how, where, when and at what rate they learn, and are responsible for their choices. Currently, in most education systems, students enter as a member of a year group (in North America this is known as a grade) and are batch processed through the curriculum choices they have made in classes linked to their year group. If we move to a student choice small credit system, students could agree with a group of peers to pursue learning together, even though they may be of different ages and at different stages. Thus, peer selection is part of personalizing the experience of learning.

What matters most here is not the form of delivery, but that students are engaged in the design of their own learning experience and that students pursue learning objectives as outlined in Chapter 3: the goals of deep and meaningful learning are unchanged. What changes is how this learning is experienced.

The Challenge

The fundamental challenges here are structural and ideological. Do schools wish to drive the choices which students can make or do they wish to be driven by the choices made by students? That is, if we moved to a system driven by the personal choices made by students, schools would need to be nimble, responsive, adaptable systems ready to accommodate a variety of choices in flexible and creative ways. We have some models for this – alternative schools (mainly aimed at students who drop out) have been working along these lines for some time. But it requires a rethink of schools as organizations. Are we ready for this?

Chapter 7: From Systems Accountability to School Based Assurance

Introduction

In this chapter, we explore the nature of accountability regimes and suggest that there is a need for a rethink of why these are in place and what they should become. While we use Alberta as a specific case, we do so because the challenges associated with the accountability regime are common across all systems which test all students at key stages of their schooling.

Key Stage Testing

Many governments in a number of OECD countries have adopted an approach to school system accountability which tested all students at key stages of their schooling so as to hold schools accountable for performance. In Alberta, for example, this has so far involved testing for all students at Grades 3, 6 and 9 as well as all students remaining in school completing their high school diploma. Similar key stage testing is undertaken in Britain. The US is now encouraging States to use standardized testing for English and mathematics.

Not all jurisdictions have followed this model. In Finland, for example, there is no key stage testing during the normal period of schooling; students' progress is measured by credit accumulation. However, Finland does have matriculation examinations which provide a bridge between the school and post-secondary education[133]. This examination is described by the National Board of Education of Finland as follows:

> The examination consists of at least four tests; one of them, the test in the candidate's mother tongue, is compulsory for all candidates. The candidate then chooses three other compulsory tests from among the following four tests: the test in the second national language, a foreign language test, the mathematics test, and one test in the general studies battery of tests (sciences and humanities). The candidate may include, in addition, as part of his or her examination, one or more optional tests. There is a separate assessment system for the matriculation examination. The tests are initially checked and assessed by each upper secondary school's teacher of the subject in question and finally by the Finnish Matriculation Examination Board.

- students often take additional time after completing their high school course requirements to prepare for matriculation. This matriculation process is seen as essential for the selection system for post-secondary places – there is strong competition, for example, for teacher education places and the examination helps identify the most able students. The strategic intent, however, is not to assess the school systems performance (accountability) by means of this examination. That is done through special studies and occasional sample based studies of particular issues.

Finland does, however, take one external assessment very seriously. That is the assessment of the systems performance against others in the OECD using PISA – the Program of International Student Assessment. Finland takes this seriously since, each time the assessment is undertaken (every three years), Finland appears best in class amongst all OECD countries. Alberta ranks very high, yet has adopted a completely different framework for accountability than its Finnish counterpart, as Pasi Sahlberg points out in his new book[134].

What Is Wrong with Key-Stage, All-Student, Testing-Based Accountability?

Stephen Murgatroyd and Neil Henry (2007) [135] developed a challenge paper which critiqued the way school boards and governments in many jurisdictions hold schools accountable. Their critique suggested that the accountability frameworks now adopted by many jurisdictions face these issues and challenges:

- **The accountability framework is reductionist** – reducing a complex system of learning to a few 'average of averages' measures. While it is accepted that not all variables can be assessed (schools are complex social networks of interactions with many layers of outputs), the outputs chosen constrain our understanding of school and student performance.
- **The accountability framework is minimalist** – in an attempt at simplicity, it unduly simplifies a complex system and in the process of doing so, loses the essence of the system. Key variables, for examples those sought by employers, are excluded. This is a similar point to the reductionist point, but it focuses on the measures not seen as relevant by the accountability pillars but which are seen as essential by other stakeholders – e.g. employers.
- **The accountability framework is combative** – since it is fundamentally used for resource allocation, performance

measurement pits one part of the system (or one school or school board) against others. While it is also used for continuous improvement, one danger of the present system (as seen in its use by the UK, for example) is that it leads to structural interventions.

- **The accountability framework is deceptive** – since the measures reduce educational activity to a few 'key' measures, it fails to recognize the importance of other factors – e.g. emotional intelligence, student engagement, community engagement – as part of the performance activities of schools.

- **The accountability framework is _not_ about the learner or learning** – the focus of the measures now used is on systems and system performance, with some reference to learning outcomes. Teacher measures and feedback, for example, are not included.

- **The accountability framework is based on a particular notion of 'trust'** – by imposing a single model of educational outcomes, the assessment process indicates that it trusts external assessment more than self-evaluation. Many accrediting bodies in the post-secondary sector, for example, have moved away from 'absolutist' criteria to self assessment process evaluation based on the vision and values of the educational organization [136]. Clearly, at the K-12 level such trust is not evident.

Murgatroyd and Henry also raised these issues:

- **One Size Does Not Fit All.** The accountability framework adopted in Alberta (and similar frameworks in use elsewhere) is not intended to address the competing needs of different stakeholders – government, school boards, school administrators, teachers, parents, and other interest groups. It is explicitly *not* intended for students. These competing stakeholder interests are not always congruent – the data collected may not reflect the interests and concerns of that stakeholder. While the data is of value *at some level* to all in the system, it is more useful as a decision support resource to some rather than others. For example, it is clearly helpful to the policy makers and funders in addressing in a narrow way the issue of "returns on its investments" in education in that it provides an efficient and independent outcome assessment which can be compared to the outcomes of other, similar jurisdictions.

- **Separating Improvement Evaluation and Accountability?** Education accountability systems have several purposes including; information to improve schools and student learning, on the one hand; and assessment of school and educational system performance on the other. At a conceptual as well as a practical level, perhaps these two purposes – evaluation aimed at school improvement and accountability - and the information collected for each should be separated: widespread and intensive but still sample based testing of key skills and knowledge for system and school district performance *vs.* internal, teacher and school, self evaluation information focused on school improvement.

- **What Gets Measured Gets Done.** In the quest for benchmarks against which one system or sub-system can compare itself to others, there has been a widespread adoption of standardized measures of output; in particular, with respect to numeracy, literacy and science. This has, in turn, led to the adoption of a standards based curriculum which gives strong emphasis to these core subjects with less emphasis on arts, creative work and other activities, such as physical activity or health. Ironically, employers, when asked, assume that core skills are present and look more for skills in collaboration and teamwork, risk taking, creativity and communications all core skills required for the rapidly developing knowledge economy. But when parental choices, resource allocation and sustainable schools appear to be partly related to performance on the accountability measures, most organizations focus on measured results. When this occurs, it is not uncommon for teachers to teach to the test.

- **Evaluating for When?** There appears to be a mismatch between educational outcomes of schools and current economic performance. For example, just as Alberta and Canada are rising in educational performance on generally accepted outcome measures of educational attainment, Canada's competitiveness is in decline – down from 12th to 16th on the World Economic Forum's Business Competitiveness Index. In part, this is a reflection of our economic structure and reliance on commodity markets for economic growth, but is also a function of our relatively low productivity both as a province and as a nation, and our failure to harness innovation. The implication is that our ability to leverage the knowledge and skills of our people is not as great as it is in other jurisdictions. There is also a sense that the skills and competency focus of the assessment and accountability framework are not in line with the skills and competencies needed for a twenty first century competitive, productive economy. This is a critical issue. As we face a war for talent, education is critical to our future as an economy provided this education fully reflects the social skills and learning required to be competitive in the new economy.

- **Predictive Validity?** Strong educational performance on educational measures in K-12 do not appear to act as predictors for subsequent educational activity – for example, despite strong performance on some key measures, Alberta has less than stellar performance on high school completion (the three year rate stands at 70.4%). Nor does student performance on formal accountability outcome measures predict subsequent learning activities. Alberta has relatively low participation rates in post-secondary education. Similar findings can be replicated elsewhere.

- **Looking in the Wrong Places?** Variations in performance *between* schools is not as great as the variation *within* schools. The implication here is that the real focus for evaluation should be on improving our understanding of why there is so much variation amongst a student population *within* a school, so that we can improve the performance of each school. Indeed, while differences between schools are not unimportant, any attempt to improve schools needs to focus on the school as a unit of measurement.

For all of these reasons, and others, there is a need to rethink the rationale for and the process of accountability in general use in school systems.

Links to the Fourth Way

When we seek to understand these concerns from a broader, more international perspective, the work of Andy Hargreaves and Dennis Shirley is helpful. Hargreaves and Shirley have spent a considerable amount of time seeking to understand the meta-patterns of educational policy adopted by governments around the world. Their book, *The Fourth Way – The Inspiring Future for Educational Change* [137], outlines distinctive phases in which governments in the developed world have sought to tackle the question of how best to 'manage' public education. Hargreaves and Shirley suggest that there have been three distinct phases in the past and that a new, fourth, way is emerging in the present.

The idea behind these four different approaches to government thinking is that as conditions change, so must policy. They see these basic streams of policy prior to the present period: (a) innovation and inconsistency (1945-1975 approximately); (b) complexity and contradiction (1975- late 1980s) – this they see as an interregnum rather than as a decisive and clear shift in policy; (c) the way of the markets and standardisation (to 1995, neo-liberalism); and then (d) performance through accountability and partnership (1995- present, modified form of New Public Management). More specifically, these phases (or "ways") look like this:

The First Way	Teachers developed their own courses and programs, often collaborating with each other. They were engaged, professional and respected. Some performed well with that freedom, but others did not. Educational outcomes varied significantly within and between schools and there were incidents of teachers using their classroom as platforms for their own unique views.
The Second Way	The way of the markets and standardisation – This is when, in the US the Reagan administration released *A Nation at Risk* and when the idea of school choice, a market for education and provincial and state curriculums and teaching standards were established. The Superintendents (In Canada and the US) and OFSTED in the UK became critical vehicles for monitoring standards. This is also when teachers started not to be trusted to take responsibility for their own teaching activities without guidance and evaluation.
The Third Way	Inspired by a variety of sources, but notably Anthony Giddens[138], governments began to see the market and centralized curriculum coupled with high stakes testing as a way to hold teachers, schools and school districts accountable for outcomes and expenditures. Ranking of schools and the identification of failing schools subject to special measures so that they can be subject to 'turn-around' measures and the special recognition of high

	performing schools were all part of this mix. Compliance rather than innovation and servant artisan teachers rather than mindful professional teachers[139] characterised the third way.
The Fourth Way	As schools become recognized for their unique circumstances – their historiographies, complexities, specialism's, challenges and opportunities – then each school is seen to have a degree of autonomy within which they can design curriculum and assessment. Balancing the needs of a system wide curriculum with local learning requires assessment which is professional, rather than bureaucratic, and schools which are accountable for their own action plans and performance commitments. A renewal of teacher professionalism is required to achieve the promise of the Fourth Way.

Alberta was an early adopter of the third way. Minister David King re-introduced diploma examinations (1984) and Provincial Achievement Tests for grades 3,6 and 9 (1982)[140]. The principles of accountability were reinforced in the first Klein-Dinning budget of 1992 and related acts and regulations, as well as through the subsequent introduction of the Government Accountability Act. While David King now indicates that the original intentions of the accountability measures he took have been "misdirected"[141], the strategy of holding public organizations accountable for measurable outcomes was strengthened throughout the period 1980-2010.

In education, the movement against the third way has gained considerable momentum from the pioneering work on *Real Learning First* by the Alberta Teachers' Association and through public consultation, resulting in the document *Inspiring Education*. However, the Government of Alberta's intentions, revealed in *Inspiring Action on Education*, do not suggest a clear path towards the fourth way. Though this strategic document focuses on student-centred education and personalized learning based on competencies, with regards to accountability, it suggests that little change is intended:

> Albertans have access to transparent, reliable and consistent ways to gauge provincial and school authority success. Alberta Education provides school authorities with meaningful information and supports to assist them in identifying areas of success and for improvement. School authorities are responsible for their results and have the flexibility to determine how they can best address the diverse needs of students. Albertans hold the education system accountable for the investment in education. Thinking differently and engaging actively in collaborative efforts with Alberta Education, partners *will further refine accountability measures and reporting mechanisms* to assure Albertans that their investment in education meets their expectations and contributes to the province's prosperity. (emphasis added)
> Government of Alberta (2010) *Inspiring Action on Education* at page 16

"Refine" is not the same as "modify" or "change" or "rethink". Like other jurisdictions, such as New Brunswick[142], the intent is to change in significant ways *what* students learn and *how* they learn but not how we hold schools accountable for learning.

Alberta is in the 'in between time' between the third and fourth ways. It will need to rethink its accountability strategy if it wishes to be a leader in the fourth way approach to managing education. In other jurisdictions, especially those focused on competencies and authentic assessment, new methods of accountability are emerging. Alberta will need to reconcile its learning intentions with its accountability practices at some point in the future if it is to truly embrace the fourth way.

Assurance, Not Accountability

More recently, a number of jurisdictions which had hitherto engaged in system-wide key stage testing as a measure of system accountability have moved away from this and are adopting a different approach. This is referred to as the transition from an accountability model to an assurance model. Behind this transition are these assumptions:

1. Not all schools have the same history, resources, catchment, intake quality, levels of teacher experience and access to technology. Each school has unique characteristics.
2. Assessing students as if they were equal because of age neglects the significant differences between students of the same age; birth order and month; intelligence and ability; parental support for learning; social supports for the student; and so on. All eleven year olds are not all equal at the point of testing.
3. For a school to be accountable for its use of public resources and its work, the school needs to own its work;

its strategic intent and purpose, its methods of teaching and its process for evaluating and supporting students.

4. Schools want to be accountable for their work and the performance of their students.

5. Schools can use sampling, teacher evaluation (when teachers are trained and supported to do this expertly) and other measures (peer evaluation, parent evaluation, self-tests) to assess performance and progress.

6. Rather than simply use a single set of measures (scores of provincial or standardized achievement tests or matriculation scores) to determine whether a school is performing, schools should provide a development plan in which it makes clear and explicit commitments for performance and then should report on progress. This is not to exclude the use of standardized tests as part of mix or measures the school chooses to use.

7. The primary level of accountability in the school system rests with professional teachers undertaking professional student assessments.

8. School boards hold schools accountable for living up to their commitments and assurances.

9. Where a school is clearly unable to meet its own commitments and intent, the school board needs to act to support the school in its plans for change.

Moving to Assurance – What is Needed

If high-stakes testing at key stages – the third way approach to accountability – is to be replaced, what should it be replaced with? The answer: school based assurance.

The idea of school based assurance is not new. There have been many developments which see such a starting point for all accountability work as critical to raising performance and improving the focus and alignment of teachers on "what matters most" within a school. The arguments in favour or school based accountability are as follows:

1. Subject to some important qualifications related to funding and capacity, schools are an appropriate unit for accountability purposes and have clear advantages compared to other possible units of accountability, such as school districts, individual teachers, and students. A school is the point of identity for students, parents and teachers. Students see themselves as part of a specific school and its culture, and we know from a variety of school effectiveness studies that a school's culture is an important variable in determining student outcomes[143].

2. As a means of rating the effectiveness of schools, value-added measures designed to measure the contribution of schools to student learning are superior to alternative measures such as average student achievement, and this conclusion holds despite the practical difficulties of implementing true value-added measures.

3. While we know little about the success of school-based assurance programs in raising student achievement, we do know that such programs can have powerful effects-both intended and unintended-on how principals behave.

An important subtext running throughout this chapter is that school-based assurance systems make most sense when schools have adequate funding and when support systems are in place to assist schools in terms of both developing accountability processes, measures and then in taking action to improve performance.

But what does school based assurance look like? During 2007 a small team, comprised of; superintendents of the Grande Prairie Public School and Livingstone Range districts in Alberta; a school trustee; some school principals; as officers of the Alberta Teachers' Association; and this author designed a framework for school based accountability that reflected the best practice of school development planning [144] and studies of school based accountability (e.g. Davis and Ellison, 2003) [145], as well as on substantial work on building quality in schools (Murgatroyd and Morgan, 1992) [146]. This framework – known as the school improvement wheel – has the following six components:

1. **Comprehensive, Critical and Reflective Self Study**
   – The self study is a data-rich, evaluation by the school and the community that looks at where it is, and at the challenges the school faces in terms of specific performance measures, as well as building skills and competencies, creating a culture and supporting learning. It explores these questions:
     • What is the school seeking to do, given its inputs, resources, community and obligations?
     • What data does the school have showing its performance on key learning outcomes, cultural metrics and other performance areas?
     • What happens when these data are weighted for inputs?

- What happens when these data are compared and contrasted with similar evidence from other schools with similar input profiles?
- What are the challenges this school has to respond to so as to improve student performance?

2. **Stakeholder Engagement**
   - Using a combination of methods (focus groups, interviews, questionnaires) and involving *all* stakeholders (school staff, trustees, government agencies, parents, pupils, local and other employers, community leaders, others ...), the school will inform its self-assessment by exploring:
     - What matters most about this school to each stakeholder group; what are the expectations and how can these be measured?
     - What is the current understanding of each stakeholder group of the performance of the school on the variables that matter to them?
     - What do stakeholders think the school is strong at?
     - What do stakeholders think the school now needs to work at to secure improvements?
     - What are the performance challenges the school needs to overcome?

3. **Peer Review and Assessment**
   - A team of peers from a different jurisdiction comes and takes a systematic look at the school – comparing the self assessment and the stakeholder

review with what they see when they are there. They offer feedback, comment and analysis based on a set of standards or rubric established before the visit, but linked strongly to the self-assessment (mission based assessment as opposed to 'abstract standards'). This may include specialists reviewing a specific area of work (e.g. mathematics, language arts) or a team of administrators looking at the school as a whole. The key task is to provide a professional, independent, mindful assessment of where the school really is and to suggest actions to improve the school's performance. Feedback made available to *all* staff and stakeholders.

4. **A School Performance Improvement Plan (or Development Plan)**
    – A detailed plan for the work of the school with clear, explicit accountability targets and commitments – but a balanced plan, not just the measures required by government agencies for key stage assessments. This plan will focus on what needs to be done to meet local and community stakeholders' expectations, trustee expectations and performance expectations set by the responsible government authority so as to ensure high performance, given the inputs to the school and resources (including teachers) available. Targets are SMART (specific, measurable, attainable, results oriented and time based). This is a public accountability statement for the school, approved by the trustees and supported by all teachers and staff of the school.

5. **Personal Improvement Plans / Professional Development**

   – Each teacher needs to review the plan and assess the implications for their own professional development and link their personal improvement plan (where they see this as appropriate)[147] to the work they will need to engage in so as to achieve the outcomes the plan commits them to. In addition, professional development resources need to be allocated in appropriate ways both at the level of the school and the district to developing those skills needed to make the plan possible.

6. **Assessment and Evidence Based Review**
   – Performance against the published plan is assessed using data and agreed measures. For key measures, triangulation (data from three different kinds of evidence) is preferred to a single 'one shot' assessment. For example, for improvements in emotional intelligence, data from a standard assessment coupled with self-evaluation and peer evaluation would be more powerful and acceptable than data from just the standard assessment. Teacher assessments and evaluations count. Data is weighted for inputs. Benchmarking is done wherever possible. This then informs the next cycle of planning.

This cyclical process, which resembles the Plan-Do-Check-Act cycle developed by W Edwards Deming[148], can be shown as follows:

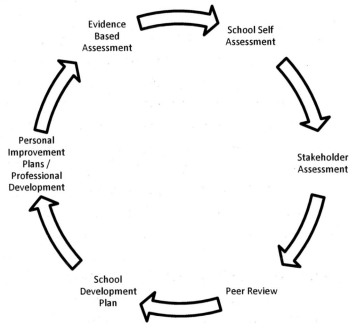

Figure Eight: School Development Planning Cycle

Many school developments plans we have seen during the last decade are vague, based on limited evidence and have little to do with seeking significant gains in performance. Some are written by principals with no reference to their community or their teaching colleagues, others are 'compromise' documents in which language is used to obfuscate challenges, minimize poor performance or set limited goals. School plans, in short, have not been seen for what they really need to be: the road-map for significant performance improvements at the level of the school; a map which has the full support of all stakeholders.

In the process of school development planning, the principles which should drive the development of this commitment document include these:

- **Integrity** – the school development planning process and the resultant plan should be developed with high standards of integrity and transparency. The school should be up front about its issues and challenges, specific about its current performance and explicit about its intended outcomes. Trust is built on the integrity of the school development planning process.
- **Comprehensive** – the plan should provide an accurate portrayal of the school 'as is (warts and all) and what the school intends to achieve. It should focus not just on the accountability requirements determined by the jurisdiction and the school trustees, but also on how the school expects to respond to other stakeholder expectations: academic, social and emotional outcomes expected by teachers, parents, pupils and the local community.
- **Focused** – to be successful, school development plans should focus on a small range of intended performance improvements (three to six major achievements) – which reflects the priorities of the school.
- **Aligned and Engaged** – The priorities and intended achievements should reflect the commitment of all staff within the school and the stakeholder community. All teachers and teacher aides should be involved in the development of the plan and committed to achieving its goals. Community consultation and engagement should be based on a genuine desire for inclusion in the process

and should reflect an understanding that the school is a critical community property and key to the future of that community.

- **Evidence Driven** – the document should not only be evidence based, but should also focus on measurable achievements. Targets, timelines and SMART (specific, measurable, achievable, realistic and time-specific) goals should be clearly laid out and the specific measures to be used to demonstrate performance should be specified.
- **Transparent** – the plan should be published on the school's web site, following its approval by trustees, and the school's performance against the plan should also be publicly available. If the plan is amended or changed – and circumstances can change quickly within a community or a school – then a change notice to the plan needs to be developed, agreed and published.

A publicly traded company is expected to file its annual performance on three key measures – profit, planet and people – and keep investors informed of changes to the operating environment and performance of the organization. Integrity and transparency are monitored by the stock exchange. Companies must also demonstrate compliance to regulations and to professional standards of practice (e.g. international accounting standards). We see the school development planning process and subsequent reporting as equivalent to this same requirement for shareholder and regulatory accountability. Both should be based on an understanding of professional integrity, public trust and transparency.

Time needs to be allocated to this work. One surprising feature of schools in Canada in general and throughout the OECD is how little time professionals are given to undertake systematic planning and systematic review. In Finland, teachers have considerably more time to undertake such work when compared to the majority of teachers. It's time to recognize that planning and accountability require investment and cannot be done 'on the fly'.

The Challenge

Moving from system wide, all students testing at key stages is a very political choice. Many politicians find such accountability for public funds essential. Yet, accountability systems are getting in the way of real learning and effective teaching, and inhibiting the transformation of our schools. Moving to an assurance model, such as is widespread in the business world for investors, makes sense. The challenge is making the change happen. One school system at a time may be the answer.

Chapter 8: Leadership and the School – Developing School Leaders for the New Renaissance

Introduction

School level leadership and systems leadership require a variety of skills and competencies. Donald Simpson, founder of The Innovation Expedition, and this author have spent a considerable part of their working lives supporting, developing and coaching leaders in organizations as varied as banks, non profits, food manufacturing, high street retail, forestry, farming, marketing and educational institutions. Our book, *Renaissance Leadership – Rethinking and Leading the Future* [149], seeks to capture our understanding of what it takes to be a leader in this 'in between time' – a renaissance age. Here this thinking is applied to educational systems and to leadership at all levels.

About Leadership

The W. K. Kellogg Foundation has been engaged in scanning activities with respect to leadership for the twenty first century. Using literature reviews, interviews, surveys, they have been exploring the question: What does leadership need to be like for the 'in between time' – an age which can be thought of as a renaissance time?

Data from this work consistently point to the notion that leadership, whether in education or elsewhere, is a means to an end, not an end in and of itself. Answering the question "leadership for what?" requires thoughtful consideration that any evaluation of effective leadership be inextricably linked to analysis of outcomes. Effective leadership is moving from hierarchical, top-down leadership models to inclusive, participatory leadership styles. Effective individual leaders are people who commit themselves to tackling challenges, help their organization and their communities articulate a vision for change, and build the commitment and wherewithal to improve the lives of people within the organization and community.

These environmental scans provide insight into current thinking about what attributes, knowledge, and skills leaders should possess to ensure their effectiveness in a global, knowledge-based, multicultural society. Future leaders, like their predecessors, must have a deep sense of mission and passion guided by strong moral, ethical, and spiritual values. Organizations and communities want leaders to reflect their vision and values for positive social change and to display courage and determination to achieve this vision.

Effective leaders are humble, self-aware, and have a high degree of accountability. They believe in the need for many people to have a seat at the table, and recognize the importance of diverse perspectives and skills. Through inclusion and charisma, they inspire confidence among many and are able to raise the level of motivation and morality among a group to help find solutions and ensure progress.

Respondents to the W. K. Kellogg surveys indicated that effective leaders must be open to change and capable of a long-term vision and a culturally sensitive world perspective. This requires continuous learning and personal development. As Shimon Peres, President of Israel, commented in an interview, leaders need to continue to learn so that they are "up to tomorrow," rather than just "up to date." He echoes the famous Wayne Gretzky quote – "you don't just need to know where the puck is, you need to know where it's going to be".

Unlike any previous time in our history, it is essential that educational leaders have the ability to master new technologies, and in particular, developments in information technology (see Chapter 5 above). Knowing how to capitalize on the advantages of evolving communications systems is essential. As Frances Hesselbein from the Peter F. Drucker Foundation remarked in an interview, "the globalization of ideas is far more powerful than the globalization of business." Information and knowledge are replacing physical resources as the most important currency in the world. Great leaders of the future will be good interpretive thinkers who know how to look at both the big picture and the micro vision and propose realistic solutions. They must be able to help their organizations and the communities in which they operate, comprehend and act on complex interconnected issues and problems with intelligence, creativity, and good judgment. They must know global and work local – what may be called being *glocal*.

Educational leaders of the future must have confidence and excellent management skills. Leaders must recognize their strengths and weaknesses and know how to build complementary teams. They should be capable of developing collaborative working relationships across numerous and varied constituencies and stakeholders. They should feel comfortable operating at all levels of society to affect and institutionalize change. Partnerships and strategic alliances are critical for effective leadership; the new leader must know how to network and build coalitions to get things done.

Looking beyond the education sector and immediate sphere of influence, educational leaders must know how to work with the others, be they corporate, government, or NGOs, because the complexity of modern problems requires that the three sectors combine resources and influence to forge new solutions. Just look at the needed and emerging response to childhood obesity or new approaches to the development of work skills for examples of such collaboration.

Finally, the educational leaders of the 21st century must have a global perspective and be willing to embrace diversity and cultural differences. Contextual demands on our leaders will require that they use a wide-angle lens and look beyond immediate boundaries and borders to solve problems. Effective leaders will encourage multiple viewpoints and will be comfortable with sharing leadership. They will know how to identify and nurture emerging leaders among them. New leaders must teach the importance of tolerance and compassion and must help people learn how to live together. To avoid multicultural conflicts, educational leaders must model multicultural acceptance and know how to leverage the value of diversity.

Renaissance Leaders are Different

We have just described the core conditions for effective and inspiring leadership for the twenty first century organizations, including educational institutions. But this description is general

– it speaks to the necessary conditions for effective leadership. Now let us look specifically at school system leadership.

For school leadership, the conditions described above are necessary, but not sufficient for renaissance leaders who wish to lead in a school or school jurisdiction. Renaissance leaders need to go beyond these necessary conditions and practice six specific skills on a systematic and regular basis for effective renaissance leadership.

What kind of leadership will offer the greatest chance in this fast changing world of harnessing the creative energy required to drive dramatic improvements in school performance, deliver a harmonious organization committed to change and improvement and enhance the quality of life for all at the school and in their local community? We believe it's a style of leadership we call Renaissance Leadership.

Renaissance leaders aren't easily described in a few neat phrases, precisely because they embody the renaissance tendency to break down rigid categories and wander into areas where the industrial mind would say they had no right to be. Consider Leonardo da Vinci, a name often invoked as the quintessential Renaissance Man. Was he a scientist, mathematician, engineer, inventor, anatomist, painter, sculptor, architect, botanist, musician, or writer? Exactly! He was all of these things, and more. Or consider Cosimo de Medici: ambassador, politician, patron of arts and architecture, banker and businessman, founder of a modern Platonic philosophical academy – and one of the lead players in the 15th century Italian Renaissance.

The renaissance leaders were thinkers; but not the type of thinker who prefers the ivory tower and indulges in thought purely for its own sake. They were thinkers with a passion for moving their ideas and knowledge to action. In a similar way, renaissance leaders in the modern knowledge economy are also people of action—but not the ready-fire-aim type of actor who believes that being fast off the mark in implementing the first plan that comes to mind is the key to success. They are self-aware people who pay attention to who they really are – what some might call their "way of being in the world"—without descending into self-absorption or losing touch with reality.

They are high integrity individuals with a passion both for driving high performance in their organizations and for helping to make the world a better place.

These modern day renaissance Leaders have a sense of history and an unusual capacity for viewing the world holistically, for practicing systems thinking, for injecting a global and a futures perspective into present challenges, for honouring diversity, and for drawing on ideas and best practices from diverse disciplines and economic sectors.

They have a capacity to function as social and technical architects designing new structures, processes and products for addressing complex challenges.

They have mastered the art of demonstrating grace under pressure, and of inspiring others to have the courage to collaborate and innovate in order to solve complex challenges.

This is because Renaissance Leaders are role models for other leaders – they have moved from being a good leader to a great leader who inspires others to lead their organizations and communities differently. Renaissance Leaders understand the future and know how they need to lead to make the future a positive one for their organization.

Renaissance Leaders Collaborate

Renaissance leaders collaborate – they understand that collaboration is the DNA of the knowledge economy. They also understand the range and scope of the collaboration required to build an effective, focused renaissance organization. They seek out:

Collaboration Among People Who Work in the Same School - Because changes are taking place in several areas of a school at the same time, all of which are interrelated, there is a need for collaboration. This is particularly true because leaders are expected to deal with these issues holistically, which means dealing with issues in an integrated fashion. A challenge today in the teaching of science will be a challenge tomorrow in the management of learning.

Collaboration Among Different Schools in the Same Region - Since changes in organizations play themselves out in at least five functional areas of work (Strategy, Structure, Systems, Skills, and Shared Values), there is an increasing need for collaboration among people from different parts of the school system in a given region. Shared learning: collaboration on cross-school challenges; collaboration on how to leverage IT for improved student performance; all represent samples of the opportunities for system wide collaboration.

Collaboration in Cross Functional Virtual Teams to Run Specific Projects - An elaboration of these two forms of collaboration reminds us that increasingly, organizations need to put together cross-functional teams to undertake specific tasks. Teams from around the world can now collaborate on projects aimed at improving school performance, as the partnership between schools in Alberta with specific schools in Finland is showing. This collaboration requires a mixed group to learn how to work together efficiently and effectively quickly and when the task is completed, they go back to their 'normal' work and a new collaborative team is formed to tackle a new task.

Collaboration with Stakeholders and Partners – Increasingly, schools as organizations concentrate on their key competencies which allow them to add high value and work out collaborative relationships with others who have high competencies in needed areas. In some cases this involves collaboration with their students, parents, community leaders and business. In other cases, another institution (college, training organization, university) may at one moment be an educational partner; at another moment a supplier of services; and at another moment these same players could be partners in designing a new educational project or service. Collaboration is dynamic and adaptive.

Collaboration with Competing Schools in a District (the concept of strategic alliances) - the building of effective clusters - Strategic alliances began in Europe in the late 1970s and early 1980s and represented an attempt by several firms in the electronic sector to save themselves from Japanese competitors during a time when the European economies were being described as sick (suffering from "Eurosclerosis", as one writer suggested). The evolving response to this crisis was to find an efficient and effective way to collaborate with former competitors to run significant projects or create a new product without having to create a merged new company or a legal joint venture. Organizations cooperated to a certain point, then took the results back to their own organizations and competed. Having learned how to organize alliances with former competitors in Europe, some firms gained the confidence to explore similar alliances with the 'enemy' companies from Asia. This concept of flexible strategic alliances found its way into various sectors, and a new range of operating principles and leadership skills emerged to support such collaborative initiatives. In education, there is sometimes felt to be competition between, say Catholic and Public schools, or between public school systems and private. However, at a regional level, all are providing education that matters through people who are passionate about learning and their students. The Renaissance Leader wants to find out how a collaboration with competitors could raise the performance of *all* in the region, and they will work with others to find out.

Public Good Collaboration Among Different Sectors of Society (for Profit, Non-profit, Public) - There is a need to help people see that concept of a collaborative culture is not just a nice thing to want to have, it is essential for the wellbeing of communities. It has become critical for economic success and social wellbeing. Many profit making companies are now seeing this collaboration as being essential for maintaining quality of life in their communities, which is essential for the economic well being of the company and for its ability to attract top level employees.

Also, this collaboration offers employees of for-profit companies great opportunities to develop badly needed leadership skills (team building, relationship building, etc.) and offers their employees opportunity to build citizenship skills—companies can't do it easily. What could a school or school system do with volunteer labour from corporations and non profits; what projects could they lead, what teaching activities could they engage in that would make a difference to the students in a school or group of schools? How can the strengths of fundamentally different organizations be harnessed in the service of learning?

New Collaborative Roles Between Employer and Employee - The new realities of a fast changing, highly competitive global knowledge economy have put severe new pressures on the conventional long term employee/employer relationship. It is now more difficult for employers to offer secure long term employment, yet more than ever they need a commitment from employees to work as if the school was their own school – they need a sense of ownership and commitment at the level of the school as an organization. All this has led to new tensions between employers, their teachers, and other adults working in the school system and has begun to inspire the creation of quite different collaborative arrangements between them. Collaboration is no longer a 'soft', HR related idea – it's a driver for building sustained, focused performance improvement in schools. Renaissance Leaders understand this and actively model collaborative behavior. Where the leader is the representative of the employer, they act so as to build this sense of ownership and commitment.

Renaissance Leaders Know How to Focus and Then Unleash Innovation

There is growing recognition of the important role of agile learning and collaboration linked to the systematic and focused work of the leader as an innovator. In our understanding, innovation is a discipline that can be taught (and learned) and that the way one structures an organization can either support innovation or impede it. School systems need to focus on recognizing that innovation is more than research—more than just a good idea. It is a good idea *that has been made to work*. That is, innovation involves a complex process that leads to activities and services that either meet a demand or create one. Meeting or creating demand requires a supply chain that involves sound educational practices and effective process and outcomes management.

When we look at innovation as a focused, systematic organizational practice, we see different types of innovation.

These include:
- technological and social innovations –e.g. using technology to help individual students review and assess their own performance and develop their learning passports for their future.
- incremental and breakthrough innovations – e.g. incrementally improving student engagement in every classroom in the school.
- innovations in strategy, structure, support systems, skills and shared values – e.g. the development of school development plans (see Chapter 7) as a way of looking at these 5 'S's in terms of how they contribute to improved

outcomes and making changes to one or more of them to enable innovation and change.

- innovation at the individual, organizational or inter-organizational level –e.g. enabling a teacher to take a risk and backing that risk, even if the 'experiment' doesn't produce the results expected. As one minister of education has said "we need more failures in our attempt at innovation – if everything we do is always 100% successful, we will never find major breakthroughs".
- innovations in learning design and student services – e.g. developing truly blended learning models which enable the student to achieve educational outcomes by working in school, at home and in their part time job using mobile learning technologies.
- process innovations (changing the way work is undertaken) – e.g. changing the way we report to parents and the community about outcomes and individual student performance.
- innovations in culture (changing the organizational structure and the operating principles including changing attitudes and behaviours) – e.g. creating a strong outcomes based (but fun) culture or using meditation to reduce the incidence of behavioural problems in a school.

To be effective, these innovations need to be:

- an executed idea—something that's gone from drawing board to implementation.
- an idea which has sustainable value—it lasts for more than a day or so as measured by performance improvements over time.

- something that makes a difference that people are willing to pay for, either directly (through price) or indirectly (by demanding the service), or which reduces costs.

Innovation can involve completely new developments—as in a breakthrough which changes the way we do things—such as the development of the internet which has changed the nature of commerce, created new opportunities for learning systems and spawned new kinds of learning support organizations. Or innovation can be an improvement on existing practices or technologies such as different ways of providing textbooks to students or a new way of providing choices to students with respect to the curriculum.

In our view, innovation is a mindset, disposition and skill set that can be taught and nurtured over time.

The Six Practices of Renaissance Leaders

There are a great many factors which shape effective leadership within a school system or school as an organization, but six key characteristics stand out as necessary conditions for renaissance leadership. Murgatroyd and Simpson (2010)[150] studied other leadership models and reviewed a total of thirty six leadership competencies which we found dominated the extensive leadership literature. They reflected on what this meant for their view of leaders in these renaissance times and identified six practices (not traits) which reflect the observed behaviour of renaissance leaders. These are:

Practice personal mastery

They have high integrity and view self-awareness as a prerequisite for leadership. They work hard to develop their capacity to innovate, and to inspire others to join them in making the world a better place. They are people others want to follow, since they show by example, integrity, honesty, passion and commitment.

Apply a glocal mindset

They have a keen sense of history and seek a holistic understanding of changes taking place on a global scale. They use this global perspective as they address local challenges and seize opportunities (global and local – hence "glocal"). In education, they are aware of key developments which make a difference to the lives, performance and well-being of students and teachers and bring this awareness to their daily practice. They recognize that you cannot simply import a solution from one country and apply it to another, but they do understand that "not everything has to be invented here".

Accelerate cross-boundary learning

They constantly seek to satisfy an intense curiosity about every facet of human life, past and present, scientific and artistic, technical and social. They guide others in distilling meaning from a morass of information, and efficiently apply their learning in creative ways to nurture innovation and drive improved performance. They don't just read and look at educational literature or attend conferences about school improvement – they try to learn about innovation, performance improvement and change from all sectors and are able to translate this work so that it has meaning for teachers, students, parents and others.

Think back from the future
They are readily able to imagine and articulate alternate futures and work back from there – connecting with lessons from the past to better understand the present and choose among possible paths to the future they see. They are not 'locked in' to the present, but can see the future of schooling in their district clearly and steer a path working back from that future to the present. They can articulate the future as a vision for students, for learning and for the school. They can make this vision real for teachers, students and parents.

Lead systemic change
They are systems thinkers who seek out patterns, inter-connections and interdependencies. They are skilled in seeking common ground and nurturing productive collaboration across diverse parts of a system – be it their own school, a school district, the education sector, a community, a network – to solve complex problems and drive large-scale change. They know how to make change happen and are used to dealing with the 'ups and downs' of the change and transformation process (see Chapter 1). They inspire followership and know how to start a movement.

Drive performance with a passion
They care that their leadership makes a substantive and sustainable difference, and are relentless in their

commitment to performance. They articulate clear (and high) expectations of themselves and others, create focused strategies for innovating to achieve these ends, and are disciplined about assessing progress. They know how to use evidence to support improvement and instill in all who work with them not just a focus on outcome, but the passion and pleasure of achievement. They know how to celebrate success and build momentum based not on rhetoric but on results. They make a tangible difference.

These six characteristics are not listed in order of importance nor are they intended to be complete – it is the list that Murgatroyd and Simpson arrived at on this stage of their expedition into the process of leadership. This list can be refined, or some key characteristics can be added, but the 'feel' of this list and its focus reflects what it will take to lead in this 'in between time'.

These ideas were developed and refined through a series of workshops at the Saïd School of Business, Oxford, with mature international leaders and have been refined in dialogue with many organizations and individuals since. Many have found this a powerful and effective starting point for a conversation about leadership in a twenty first century organization - exactly as we intended.

Some have observed that the key characteristics of renaissance leaders are deceptively simple to list but difficult to practice daily. Others have suggested that keeping the list of six characteristics close to hand helps them be better leaders daily. Our intent, in offering this thinking, is to challenge people to think about a simple question: "What kind of leadership does a renaissance educational organization need, and how can the key characteristics of these leaders best be captured?"

The Challenge

School leaders are often called "administrators", and increasingly the bureaucratic burdens of school management get in the way of their ability to lead and drive performance with passion. The big challenge is: How we can cut the red tape and focus on what matters most; making schools a great place to be, work and play for all adults and students which, as a result of the passionate pursuit of performance, lead to great results for all?

Not an easy challenge.

Chapter 9: The School, The "System" and Governance

Introduction

In 2000, John Carver formalised the proposal he had been working with for some time that school boards – locally elected trustees, known in Britain as Local Education Authorities (LEA's) – needed reform[151].

A radical redesign of the function of school boards, Carver explained, would include (1) a focus on educational results rather than on the methods by which they were achieved, (2) newly defined relationships with the general public and parents, and (3) a commitment on the part of the board to speak with one voice rather than as a group of individuals with individual agendas.

His reform agenda, which many jurisdictions adopted, assigns the school superintendent a role parallel to that of the CEO in a corporation. Carver says the role of the school board is "to govern the system, rather than run it." He also has suggested that school boards have traditionally micromanaged the educational process, something that would spell doom for any manager in a business setting, and sees the superintendent as the captain of the ship, making decisions day to day, with the trustees as the owners of the ship, looking only at how well the ship is doing in terms of outcomes.

The context for Carver's agenda was that many school trustees felt that they could impose "solutions" on school systems which reflected their own ideological assumptions about education.

They could determine the balance of curriculum, determine which text books could and could not be used, what books the library could and could not have, which technologies schools should use and who could and could not be hired. Superintendents, in some jurisdictions at least, felt that they competed with trustees in terms of who made decisions. Carver was right to seek reform.

One district that was quick to follow Carver's prescription was Colorado. An independent review[152], conducted just two years after the Carver based changes, saw that the school boards were better able to focus on policy issues and that superintendents were better able to carry out the day-to-day operations for which they were responsible.

Three basic models dominate governance in the developed world's public school systems. These are:

1. Regionally (where a region can be a city, a conurbation, a county or some other grouping of schools) elected trustees who are tasked with the work of overseeing a group of schools and being accountable for expenditure and performance.
2. Regionally (where a region can be a city, a conurbation, a county or some other grouping of schools) appointed trustees who are tasked with the work of overseeing a group of schools and being accountable for expenditure and performance. In this model, Mayors (or equivalent) appoint trustees and take an active role.
3. Direct funding and accountability from the State/Province or national Government to individual schools – an

increasing feature of the system operating in England and Wales.

Several studies have shown that, at least with respect to the first two of these models, they make little difference to student outcomes. One major study, which looked at governance reform in nine cities, says this[153]:

> While school leaders tout many improvements in test scores, attendance and graduation rates, in fact, we were unable to establish conclusively that the change in governance had any causal relationship to improved performance, or that, using nationally-normed test data, our cities had greater improvements than anywhere else.

But while Carver's "hands-off at the trustee level and power to the Superintendent" focus has dealt with one aspect of governance (and this, too, now needs reform), it has not dealt with the other substantial issues: (a) the role of the government (state, provincial or national, depending who has the funding role); and (b) the relative power of the system versus the school.
A mantra for this chapter is simple: The governance structure "is not a solution, it is an enabler...creat[ing] possibilities for the kind of bold leadership needed" for the transformation and reform of school systems"[154].

The Role of the Government

Governments who provide funds to schools and school systems have a legitimate right to and a direct accountability for the expenditure of these funds. They also have a significant role of stewardship (setting direction for the system as a whole), since they are seeking to create the necessary conditions for communities, families, entrepreneurs, social agencies, business and others to be successful and sustain their jurisdiction against fierce competition for capital, culture and people from others. Education is a major investment and those that make this investment have rights.

Governments should not, however, seek control and engage in intervention at the level of the school – they are system stewards, not school controllers.

Here are the five key functions of funding government departments or ministries with respect to education:

1. To provide funds to enable equitable access to educational services and supports for all eligible students (defined by law in terms of school start and leaving dates for compulsory schooling) and to ensure that this funding supports those students who have special needs. This includes: capital expenditure; expenditure on technology infrastructure; bussing; teacher salaries; and the operating costs of the school system. Such funding should be based on seeking to secure equitable outcomes and should reflect regional differences in access and social conditions.

2. To establish the broad framework for the learning outcomes of the educational system. That is, rather than detailed curriculum objectives for each year (or grade) for each subject, outcomes should be set to be achieved at key stages, provide support for professional educators to develop appropriate strategies for ensuring that these outcomes can be met, and invest in teacher professional education to enable curriculum development.

3. To set the governance framework for public education: define the role of school boards, trustees, superintendents and school leadership so that there is no doubt about the decision making process with respect to education.

4. Define the parameters of public assurance for educational outcomes and the methods by which these outcomes will be assessed. That is, as we saw in the chapter on accountability, create the framework for school based assurance systems, define the quality assurance measures that need to be incorporated into school development plans (e.g. sampling of students on standardized tests, special studies of issues which emerge at the system level, participation in PISA and so on).

5. Set the standards for teacher qualifications – defining the conditions which need to be met for a person who can be permitted to give credit for students who complete a program of study or an activity which is credit worthy – and define how these standards will be achieved, including making investments in teacher initial education and in ongoing professional development.

Sounds simple. But this is a demanding and difficult list of things to do. But notice something about it: it is not about control. It is about setting direction and getting out of the way, especially in terms of day to day governance and curriculum.

It is also about respecting the professionalism of teachers. Teachers receive a substantial professional education. They should be able, then, to develop appropriate learning strategies and resources to deliver to the key outcomes set by government.

It should not be the work of government to define when a student studies a particular thing or engages in a specific activity, nor should it be up to government to determine which text books (if any) a school or a teacher may use to achieve a certain outcome. The government role is to 'steer not row'.

The government may engage with local trustees or boards in negotiations about funding. The idea of a flat fee following the student has been attractive to some politicians – it is the basis of voucher schemes. But it is a poor way to think about the complexity of the system. To give just four examples:

- A student born in the town of Field in British Columbia, Canada, can receive a quality elementary education in that town but has to be bussed to a different town to receive their secondary (junior high and high school) education – Field is simply not big enough to support this level of schooling and the students are bussed to Golden (55 km away). The costs of rural education and of maintaining a rural school system are different from the cost structure of a large urban area.
- Aboriginal students living on reserve are known to have challenges with respect to learning, not least of which is relative poverty and considerable challenges with respect to health. If governments seek to secure the same educational outcomes for aboriginal students as for their urban non-aboriginal citizens, then funding for aboriginal education needs to be substantially greater than for their counterparts in non-aboriginal communities.
- Special needs students, depending on their assessed learning and support needs, require support over and

above the baseline funding given to those students designated as 'normal' (sic).

- Making an initial investment in technology is a relatively straightforward matter – but the greening and support costs are often greater than the costs of the initial investment. Lifecycle costing and investment is needed to make initial technology investments work.

Funding is not a simple matter and is often a matter of significant disputes. Indeed, in the US, legal action by parents and cities against states has resulted in major challenges to the basis of funding of educational systems[155].

When government seeks to get directly involved in the affairs of specific schools, for example in failing schools' strategies, government enters a zone of inevitable failure. A school may be failing in comparison to some absolute standard or in comparison to some analysis of average performance of all schools in a jurisdiction, but given the nature of students coming to the school and the nature of the social conditions, it may be an outstanding success. Seeking equity of outcomes and creating the conditions which give each school the best opportunity to succeed is the role of Government.

The Role of Local School Boards

Now let us look at the local level; the community level. Different countries have sought different solutions to the question of community engaged in the management of education. In the US, for example, there has been an ongoing battle between cities and states with respect to education. Governors have, often times, ceded control of some key educational decision making to mayors who in turn have created mechanisms for local engagement, appointing boards of education and education CEOs who sit in the mayors' cabinets.

In Canada, there is a very different tradition. Let us look at Edmonton as an example. Every so often (usually every three years, but on rotation), the citizens of the City of Edmonton elect two sets of school trustees – one for the public system and one for the separate (Catholic) system. Trustees are elected on the basis of a geographic distribution – by Ward. These trustees are accountable in law for the work of the schools in their jurisdiction. Each school board (one Public and one Catholic) appoints a superintendent, shapes the educational strategy, and is responsible for the appointment of educational leaders in the schools in their district. These superintendents, working with the board, craft policy which guides the work of schools.

This same process is followed in some fifty eight jurisdictions in Alberta[156], though not all communities have both a public and separate school system (some communities are too small to support parallel school systems).

Funding for schooling comes from a local tax levy, in addition to government grant funding, which every citizen pays. Additional funding can be raised by school boards through fund raising activities or user-fees.

What should school boards do, given the role identified for government above? Their key responsibilities should be these seven activities:

1. Set a clear, focused educational framework for achieving the outcomes set by government which fully reflect local conditions. This framework may add outcomes which reflect local needs and conditions or interpret government set outcomes in a specific way to reflect local conditions.
2. Hire a superintendent of schools and other key district leadership officers and hold them accountable for achieving goals set by the school board.
3. Approve for each school their school development plans and models of assurance, so that they can review school outcomes.
4. Allocate funds to support the work of the school system, making sure that funds are directed to enable the achievement of objectives.
5. Review annually the assurance reports of each school; what have they achieved in terms of their own school development plan, and what adjustments do these give rise to for the plan; and what has been achieved at a system level according to the superintendent.
6. Understand future trends and challenges and develop strategic plans for the system as a whole which will inform school development plans and the functioning of the district.
7. Celebrate, with their entire school system and the community, educational achievements and the work of schools and keep this work in the forefront of the minds of citizens.

Some may suggest that some of these activities give boards too much work with respect to individual schools and creates a dangerous basis for trustees to get overly involved at the level of the school. This is not the intention here. The intention is to move from accountability to assurance, but the assurance model requires oversight. What the trustees are looking at when they look at a school development plan or are reviewing the results of the work of the school are these questions:

- Does the plan have integrity and is it comprehensive? Will it enable the school to achieve the outcomes it has set for itself and are required of it by government and the school board?
- Are the resources available to the school adequate to undertake the work outlined in the school development plan?
- What supports can the board or the community in general offer to the school to help it achieve the plan it has developed?

What they are not engaged in is any form of operational management review or teacher assessment or analysis of administrative performance. Such issues are between the superintendent and the staff of the school. Nor are they looking at whether a particular school is teaching a particular subject in a particular way – this is a matter for the school itself. What the trustee is charged with is a requirement to assure the public that all of the schools in the system are on track to achieve what each of the schools has said they would do and that appropriate investments have been made by the board to make that happen.

This model could give cause for concern, with trustees wanting to get really into the school development planning process. They should not. The trustee is in the role of a regulator not a facilitator. As a regulator they are asking the questions outlined above, the basis of which is "is this a quality plan to achieve the outcomes set?" That's it.

How a board functions with this agenda is a matter of concern. Carver's model has operated for some time across the Canadian system and has created a powerful role for superintendents. Some boards rarely discuss educational issues, but do look at funding, school closures, and policies with respect to hiring and so on.

School boards must be engaged in a conversation and policy role with respect to the framing of the work of schools – educational strategy. They should not be involved in detailed discussions about curriculum at the level of detail. For example, one superintendent has committed all of its schools to a focus on 21st century skills as a basis for all teaching and curriculum delivery. This may or may not be a good thing, but the board itself was never engaged in a conversation about whether or not this was desirable. They should be, so that they understand the implications and the challenges of implementation. But they should not be in a position to go to the next step and look at the implications of this subject by subject or school by school. The schools themselves will do this in their school development plans.

Some modifications now seem appropriate to the ways in which boards work and the respective roles of superintendents or CEO's of education. (As an aside, it may also be time to change the language associated with this key role in the system – "superintendent" reflects a particular kind of system, the term "chief education officer" may be better suited to the system now emerging. Language sends signals and carries implications!).

Boards shape strategy and set the framework for the work of schools. Superintendents advise boards and make strategy happen by supporting schools in the development of appropriate, focused and meaningful school development plans. They coordinate and collaborate with school based leaders, rather than control them. The most important thing they do is appoint the principals of schools and support them in their school development planning work.

Superintendents are also problem solvers, networkers and future thinkers. They are the key renaissance leaders (as described in Chapter 8) in the system and need to demonstrate the leadership behaviours associated with this responsibility.

But superintendents are accountable to the board. The board agrees upon annual and medium term objectives and a personal learning agenda with the superintendent and reviews performance annually. The board sets the framework for educational strategy in the district and holds schools accountable for their own assurance framework and their development plans. The board does so on the basis of collective responsibility, but is seeking to challenge the system to be the best it can be with the resources available to achieve the outcomes expected. It should see itself as liable for any system failure within its jurisdiction – a failure to achieve the outcomes expected. It should govern itself accordingly, using modern methods of board functioning.

The School as the Centre for Decision Making – The Empowered School

The centre for the real work of an educational system is the school. It is the organization on which everyone associated with education focuses, since it is where learning happens and where performance occurs.

A principle developed in the practice of total quality management, including in schools[157], is that all key decisions should be made nearest to the student. Key decisions about: the work of learning and the practice of teaching; how key learning outcomes can best be achieved; and how progress in learning can best be assessed, need to be made by those nearest to where these issues really mean something. While these decisions can be informed (evidence based decisions, best practice informed) they need to be glocal decisions.

This puts a burden on the staff of the school, but then they are professionals. Just as doctors and lawyers interpret evidence, best practice in the light of the client or patient in front of them, teachers need to do the same with their students. What will be best for them, given what we are seeking to achieve and where this student is on their learning journey? Teachers and their school based colleagues are best positioned to make professional judgements about what will make a difference to the learning outcomes for the students in their care. We should both enable them to do this well, and trust them to do this work themselves.

What does this require at the level of the school from a governance perspective? It requires these five things:

1. A principal who is respected by his or her own staff and supported by the superintendent who acts as an educational leader. Never satisfied with current performance; always striving for improvement; passionate about learning, performance and education; and skilled at leading change. A renaissance leader in action.

2. Staff who are aligned around a school development plan which they each have a hand in developing and which commits them to measurable outcomes, and who are dedicated to performance and passionate about learning. The school should be selecting its own staff and investing in their development.

3. School based budgeting which permits the school to move funds and resources according to need in real time, with these decisions being linked to the achievement of the outcomes outlined in school development plans.

4. A performance and outcome focused school which sees achieving outcomes not as a distraction but as *the work*, and has fun and generates energy in doing so. It sees outcomes at the level of each student, each group of students, and at each key stage as its challenge and opportunity. It celebrates achievements at all levels all of the time. It has appropriate methods of assessment, assurance and accountability in place so that it can demonstrate for itself, its community and others that it is doing what it said it would do; the basis of assurance.

5. A school which engages parents, students and the community in its work, especially the work associated with school development plans and assurance.

This list does not take up a lot of space, but for many schools this is a radical agenda. Many schools do not have development plans which reflect the engagement process implied here nor do they have appropriate methods of assessment. Many communities do not feel in touch or welcome in schools and others would suggest that assessment by schools of their own work is an emerging and growing activity, not yet fully mature. Not all school systems permit school based budgeting with movement between budget lines, although this is what is needed to permit truly flexible responses to the emerging issues within a school.

Nonetheless, these five requirements are the key to building a governance system which puts learners and teachers at the heart of the work of the system, and empowers those nearest the student to make decisions in real time in the best interest of that student, and of the education system of which they are a part.

A considerable body of work on school effectiveness showed that the leadership and the culture of the school were the critical variables in determining differential performance between schools. The governance framework outlined here demands that these two variables be built upon to enable performance gains at the level of the school. Performance is not a system phenomenon; it is an artefact of what happens every day in classrooms in every school. We need to enable this level of the system to act quickly, responsibly and effectively to constantly improve performance.

Refocusing the Governance System

What has been outlined in this chapter is a refocusing of the system from a top-down accountability model to a bottom-up assurance model. In the Figure Nine below, we show the present system on the left and the system as proposed here on the right. This new system sees students, teachers and schools as where the real ability lies for performance, and therefore where most decision authority should rest; everyone else sets context, provides framing and supplies resources.

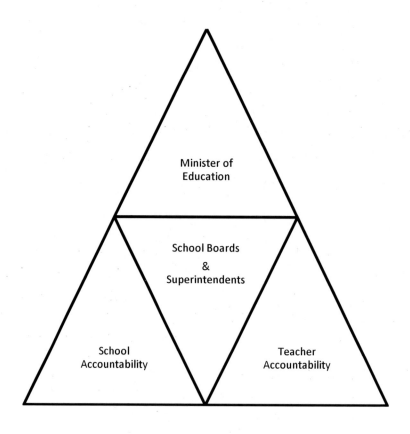

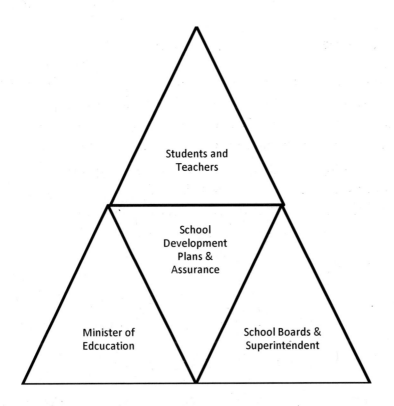

Figure Nine: The Old Framework of Governance (Left) and the New Assurance Based Model (Right)

In reality, the two systems outlined in Figure Nine will co-exist and a kind of 'plate tectonics' will emerge which permits the gradual transition from left to right over time. But placing students at the heart of the work of the system is everyone's mantra (generally rhetoric), so the proposals in this chapter (already existent to some extent in many school systems) are about turning rhetoric into reality.

The Challenge

Attempts to change governance are political. The politics of these changes are very tough, especially in highly successful systems. "If it isn't broke, why fix it?" is the current cry from many who have the power to make such decisions. In answer to those objections, there are two reasons to make this shift. The first is that we are generally, in advanced societies, moving from the third way to the fourth way (see Chapter 7) in terms of how we manage public services and understand the respective roles of the actors in a system. The second is that our current system of governance is inhibiting the performance opportunities for schools; schools could do better with the kind of freedom and authority envisaged here – Finland being an example of a system which is close to that outlined here and a consistent top performer in any measure of system success.

The challenge is how do we get from where we are to where we need to be?

Once while in Ireland, I asked directions from a particular location in Drumcondra to the train station in central Dublin. I was told by my amused Irish colleague, "if I were you, I wouldn't start from here!". That may be the challenge here. There are many egos invested in the current system. Asking them to let go and cede control to others may be difficult. But if we are serious and passionate about performance, a change is needed. So we have to start from here.

Chapter 10: Schools and the New Renaissance

Introduction

We began this book with an understanding of some of the dynamics of change taking place in society, which led us to the suggestion that schools need to change. The focus was on three major themes; 'we can do better'; new demands arising from the economy; and technology. We also mentioned that our students are changing.

The core argument made in Chapter 1 was that we are in an in-between time between one kind of socio-economic society (the information age) and another (the robotic-biotechnology age), something which will have become evident in your reading of Chapter 5, which explored the technological developments occurring now.

In this final chapter, I want to connect this thinking to the view of the new renaissance Donald Simpson and I have been exploring for considerable time. In particular, I want to connect the idea that changing schools, teaching and learning is an essential response to the new renaissance we are experiencing.

Why Renaissance?

The term "renaissance" has an interesting history. It was not until the nineteenth century that the French word *"renaissance"* achieved popularity in describing the various cultural movements that began in the 13th century. It was first used in this way by the French historian Jules Michelet in 1855 and was made popular by the work of Jacob Burckhardt (1818-1897), especially with his book *The Civilization of the Renaissance in Italy* which, though originally published in 1860, remains a classic description of the Italian renaissance 1350-1550.

During the medieval renaissance, people found the courage to:

- Challenge generally accepted boundaries of thought and behaviour
- Explore and discover new areas – physically, mentally, artistically
- Question long held beliefs and traditional organizational structures – political, religious, social, artistic
- Develop a different and broader vision of themselves
- Create new ways of expressing themselves, of describing the world, and of addressing the challenges faced by that world

- and these developments signified a shift from one world order to another – the renaissance was a 'tipping point' or a response to the 'in between time' then being experienced.

In this book, I am using the term "renaissance" as a powerful rallying call for creative change in periods of major paradigm shifts. This language gives support to those leaders who are moved to action by awareness of the lessons from earlier renaissance periods and by a desire to emulate the behaviour of some of these leadership heroes from an earlier age.

The world has seen many "renaissances"; literally periods of rebirth, rejuvenation or reawakening in which a spirit of courageous, creative, open inquiry inspires breakthroughs in the arts, sciences, technology and business. This type of leadership in periods of major change ultimately leads to fundamental changes to economic, political and social models. Our understanding of these times draws particularly on lessons from an iconic historical Renaissance in Europe and uses them to inspire modern day renaissance leadership; mindful that renaissances have occurred and continue to occur in many non-European environments. We need to draw on these experiences also to influence our thinking and shape our actions.

One renaissance figure many are familiar with is Leonardo da Vinci. He was a polymath, interested in many aspects of the world – science, engineering, art, music, botany, architecture, mathematics. He made his early living through music and his later living through art. He was curious about everything around him and his curiosity led him to systematic inquiry. He was engaged in the active pursuit of his interests. He did not just imagine or think about things, he did them. For him, the leap from thinking to doing was a very short one. Finally, he used all of his senses as a way of deepening his sensitivity to the world around him and as a means of sharpening his responses to that world. Da Vinci was a renaissance man.

A modern renaissance man was Peter Drucker, who died in 2005 after a glorious career as a business educator and writer. The thirty-nine books he wrote between 1939 and his death, together with his many public lectures and seminars show us, as Jeffrey Krames observes in his book *Inside Drucker's Brain*, that he was "the ultimate renaissance man". Drucker showed great interest in the early work of the Innovation Expedition aimed at strengthening the nonprofit sector. He honoured us by loaning us his most powerful brand (his name) and challenged us to identify, inspire, and celebrate outstanding leadership in Canadian nonprofits. We did this for 12 years through the Peter

F. Drucker Foundation for Non Profit Innovation, led by my colleague Dawn Ralph.

Peter Drucker provides the starting text for our view of the modern renaissance. He observed: "we are now in another critical moment: the transition from the industrial to the knowledge economy. We should expect radical changes in society as well as in business". Through our work on renaissance leadership we continue to utilize and celebrate what Peter taught us, and we commit ourselves to introduce this amazing human being to a new generation of young leaders who do not know him.

The modern view of "renaissance" is that it refers not to a particular time in history or events in a particular location but to a series of events, some of which are contradictory or paradoxical. It refers to significant and irreversible change in the way society views art, itself and others and how individuals relate to each other. Also involved is a change in the role of institutions and a different role for science and religion. In short: it's a description of a period of flux in which some of the fundamentals of society change. This is an excellent description of our world now; a world in which established norms can change suddenly and unexpectedly, as anyone living in Egypt or Greece or Italy or Ireland will tell you.

Characteristics of the 'Old' Renaissance

The world has seen many 'renaissances'. Various periods in the histories of many regions can be seen to fit this description; England, Germany, France, Spain, Netherlands, Poland, and many eastern European countries claim a renaissance. They each experienced different events, influences and changes, but common to them are these seven elements:

1. Changes in understanding of the nature of a nation state and the way in which its citizens relate to it.
2. A revival of an interest in the past. In the medieval period, this focused on antiquity and the lessons that could be learned from a better understanding of it.
3. A strong and abiding interest in science and technology.
4. Changes in the patterns of trade and commerce, bringing with it new understandings of the world and the 'way the world works'; especially in terms of cultural differences.
5. An understanding of the importance of the arts (painting, sculpture, theatre, literature, design) in shaping communities and its leaders.
6. The emergence of new institutions and new alliances.
7. A changed view of the way in which man relates to nature; largely informed by advances in scientific thinking and philosophy.

The idea of a renaissance is about a focus on changes in worldview and meaning, rather than just events in a particular location over a particular time.

A Modern Day Renaissance

We are living through a renaissance period now. Whether in North America, Europe, China, India, Brazil or the United Arab Emirates, this is a different time from that experienced in these same places in the 1970s and 1980s.

In the early 1960s, Peter F. Drucker, original thinker that he was, wrote down and published what a small core of perceptive leaders were already talking about: the idea that the emergence of knowledge as a key economic resource was beginning to spark a period of fundamental change around the globe.

Fast-forward to 2008, and see how the authoritative but often dusty tomes of *Encyclopedia Britannica* have ceded the field to an upstart, free compendium of knowledge called Wikipedia; written collaboratively by anyone with an Internet connection and a desire to contribute. It has more than 75,000 active contributors, working on more than 10 million articles in more than 150 languages, and is used by at least 700 million visitors around the world each year. This demonstrates a major shift in how we create, collect, store and access knowledge.

Clearly, we are living through another historical period of major change. We are throwing off the shackles of the industrial era, with its mechanical models, strict hierarchies, division of labour into silos, and command-and-control leadership, and exploring the appropriate operating principles for the global knowledge economy. We are now also beginning to transition from an information age within this knowledge economy to an age of robotics and biotechnology (see Chapter 1).

One safe assumption behind all our efforts to support the development of renaissance leaders is that we are living through a new swing point in history. The new age began somewhere around 1970 with the coming together of a host of new realities (social and cultural, technological, economical, ecological, and political). Some of the key drivers of change for this new era are:

- **A great increase in global competition** — at the end of World War II, North America's economy was the only one not badly hurt by the war. Now the competition is global. The re-building of Europe and Japan was followed by amazing developments among the Asian 'Tigers' (Thailand, Malaysia, Korea and others), and more recently by the BRIC countries (Brazil, Russia, India and China). Now competition is clearly global.

- **The changing nature of competition**—competition is no longer dependent primarily on cheap electricity and raw materials. It is now more dependent on an educated workforce, an infrastructure for organizing and sharing information, and entrepreneurial leaders with a capacity to motivate, integrate, collaborate and inspire others.
- **An explosion of new technologies**—particularly information and communication technologies (computerization, miniaturization, digitization, satellite communication, fibre optics and the Internet).
- **The emergence of global capital markets**—this is a dramatic change (made possible by the new communication technologies). This change is not high in the consciousness of most people, but it led to a dramatic shift in the way business is conducted, to the globalization of business, and to a significant shift in the nature and extent of competition.
- **A dramatic change in demographic patterns**—both in terms of the aging of population and of the shift in major population growth from developed to the developing countries. In particular, the shift in the middle class dominance from North America and Europe to Asia, India, and China; which is rapidly occurring and changing social and economic dynamics.

An increasingly common description for this new age is "the global, highly competitive, fast changing knowledge-based economy". The arrival of this new economy has sparked a global, organizational revolution over the past quarter century. The world emerging from this revolution is unlike any known before. No longer are the only key assets for business the classical ones of raw materials and cheap labour. Most of the old criteria for organizational success have been turned upside down. Now key assets are: a highly-educated workforce; knowledge; and the entrepreneurial collaborative, and innovative leadership needed to utilize this knowledge.

Policy-makers and business organizations throughout the world now find themselves in the position of needing to:

- figure out the new kind of economic game we are playing; understand the rules of this new game;
- develop the strategies and skills that will allow them to function successfully in the fast-changing game; and
- get themselves in condition to play the game energetically and enthusiastically.

These kinds of new economic challenges are not simply a problem to be faced by companies relying on international trade. They affect all firms, in any country, as the 'playing field' is now global, and is based on knowledge as a critical resource. They also affect all who deliver education and knowledge skills, since this is now the most valued asset for any society: education has become the cornerstone of competitive advantage, whether of firms, nations or communities. Schools are therefore in the front line of the new renaissance.

The new renaissance, then, directly affects many aspects of our lives; our health care and education systems, our social services, and our arts and culture activities all depend on the revenue obtained from the income of the market sector. Only nations that continue to create new wealth can sustain high-quality physical, social and cultural environments.

Signs and Signals of a New Renaissance

If the previous sections described the drivers of change, what then are the signs and signals that a modern day renaissance is indeed underway? We are seeing:

Fundamental change in how people define and relate to their community: The emergence of social networks driven by like-minded individuals and groups linked by technology is redefining our notions of community and involvement. Blogs (web documents created instantly by anyone) are becoming focal points for news and information. Facebook, LinkedIn, and MySpace connect millions of people with shared interests across time and space. YouTube is the new television, and iPods and iPads the vehicles for music and film sharing across boundaries. The ubiquitous cell phone is giving personal interconnectivity a new meaning. Specialized communities to create new goods and services can be established in seconds and begin transactions in minutes.

Artifacts that symbolize a changed understanding of the world: Art, music, architecture, texts, three-dimensional sculptures, and historiographies are all appearing which represent cross-cultural, inter-generational thinking; symbolizing the 'flattening' of the world through instant communication. In Dubai, the world's first continually shape-shifting apartment building has been designed; changing our very notion of a building, and demonstrating the power of imagination when combined with the ability to create incredibly complex technology.

Challenging of taken-for-granted assumptions and orthodoxy in general, particularly in science, technology, and nature: The ability to manipulate genes to change the structure of matter and the nature of plants; learning how to clone living things and grow embryos; the capacity to predict biological development, including individual susceptibility to specific illnesses—all these challenge our assumptions about the relationships between science and development and science and society.

Shifts in the geographic locus of knowledge and power: Dubai and Qatar are fast becoming the new financial centres for certain kinds of financial services. Qatar is the fastest growing economy in the world. Brazil, Russia, India, and China (the so-called BRIC economies) are fast emerging as new economic engines in the world economy and starting to challenge the established G8 economies. As they do so, the locus of economic power is shifting. Mumbai is an established innovation centre for technology in the same way that regions in the Middle East (especially the UAE, Kuwait, and Qatar) and China are emerging as leaders of green technology innovation in practice. Singapore is leading in stem cell biology; Silicon Valley in software development. More of these centres of excellence will emerge over the next 25 years, few of them located near the current centres of power. The geography of innovation is changing.

New gatekeepers of knowledge/authority and a global leveling of the playing field: Universities used to be the keepers of knowledge and the cradle of knowledge development. Increasingly, people are looking to new knowledge networks—clusters and networked centres of excellence and corporate academies—for ideas and innovation. Innovation is flowing rapidly across boundaries. The role of private capital in fostering innovation and knowledge development is becoming more critical.

The world is changing quickly. We hold that the emerging renaissance cannot be undone. History shows us once the dynamics of a renaissance have taken hold, there can be no turning back of the clock. The patterns that will shape power, knowledge, culture, economy, society for the next hundred years are being set right now.

Our Schools are the Cornerstone of the New Renaissance

Understanding these dynamics and providing a personal and social basis for responding to them is the key underlying work of schools.

What does this mean?

All of the ideas and suggestions for change made in this book are responses to this idea. From rethinking the design and role of schools, looking differently at curriculum, learning and teaching and leveraging technology to rethinking accountability and governance are all responses to the challenges of positioning a community or nation in the new renaissance.

New forms of leadership are also required which reflect the capacity schools need to have to be nimble, lean, responsive, flexible, creative and inspiring. From superintendents, principals, student leaders and all who seek to make a difference, values driven leadership informed by an understanding of this broad context in which change is taking place is essential for the focused development of high performing school systems. And performance counts. The renaissance described here has some harsh challenges. Schools that fail their students in terms of enabling students to develop resilience, skills and understanding needed for the renaissance age and the new economy will be failing a generation of community members; the stakes are high.

Experience gained through working with educators for over forty years gives me confidence that (often despite the system in which they work) classroom teachers and school based leaders are best able to respond to the challenges faced by students, parents, and communities faced with the challenges the new renaissance is throwing at them. By collaboration, such leaders can make a real difference. The task of all others in the school system is to enable this work to occur in the most productive and effective way possible.

The Challenge

The new renaissance poses challenges and presents possibilities. It will take courage, passion and commitment to secure the advances in schooling and learning that we know are now both needed but are also possible.

Hope abounds. The Royal Society of Arts and Manufacturing, in its commitment to this agenda, founded a school in Tipton, Cheshire, England, which practices many of the ideas and recommendations made in this book. Its work is now being emulated by over two hundred and fifty other schools in the UK and across Europe. Innovation and change is possible and sustainable. The challenge is to start the journey and not be discouraged when challenge, threat or change occurs.

Renaissance leaders are tenacious and determined. Show us that you are one of them.

Notes and References

Preface

[1] I wrote about this work recently. See Murgatroyd, S. *These Special Needs Learners Shaped My Life*. (2010) http://www.ldexperience.ca/these-%E2%80%98special-needs%E2%80%99-learners-shaped-my-life-by-dr-stephen-murgatroyd/ [Aug. 21, 2011]

[2] Reynolds, D, Sullivan, M and Murgatroyd, S (1987) *The Comprehensive Experiment*. London: Falmer Press.

[3] There are several articles, but see: Murgatroyd, S (1992) "A new Framework for Managing Schools – Total Quality Management." *School Organization*, Volume 12(2), 175-200; Murgatroyd, S (1984) "Relationship Change and the School." *School Organization*, Volume 4(2), 171-178; Murgatroyd, S and Reynolds, D (1984) "The Creative Consultant – The Potential of Consultancy as a Model of Teacher Education." *School Organization*. Volume 4(4), 321-335. A full list is available from Taylor & Francis, publisher.

[4] Murgatroyd, S. and Morgan, C (1992) *Total Quality Management and the School*. Milton Keynes: Open University Press.

[5] See www.galileo.org

[6] Murgatroyd, S and Simpson, D (2010) *Renaissance Leadership – Rethinking and Leading the Future*. New York: Lulu Press.

Chapter 1

[7] Shanghai and Hong Kong are not countries – the remainder of the top ten are.

[8] *Shaping Alberta's Future – Report of the Premiers Council on Economic Strategy*. (May 2011), 74-75.

[9] Alberta Teachers' Association. *Looking Forward – Emerging Trends and Strategic Possibilities for Enhancing Teaching and Learning in Alberta Schools, 2009-2012*. (Edmonton, AB, 2010).

[10] Alec.co.uk, *Top Ten Most Popular Careers*. <http://www.alec.co.uk/free-career-assessment/top-10-most-popular-careers.htm>[June 5th 2010].

[11] Government of Alberta (2009) *Measuring Up – Progress Report on the Government of Alberta Business Plan*.

[12] Murgatroyd, S and Couture, J.C. *Using Technology to Support Real Learning First in Alberta Schools*. (Edmonton, AB: The Alberta Teachers' Association, 2010).

[13] Meteri Group and the University of Calgary *Emerge – One to One Lap Top Learning Initiative – Year One Report*. (Edmonton, AB: Government of Alberta: Ministry of Education, 2009).

[14] Government of Alberta (2009) *Measuring Up – Progress Report on the Government of Alberta Business Plan.*

[15] Government of Alberta finance and enterprise website.

[16] Tapscott, 1995; Partnership for 21st Century Skills. (2008) *21st Century Skills Education and Competitiveness.* http://www.21stcenturyskills.org/documents/21st_century_skills_education_and_competitiveness_guide.pdf (Tuscon, AZ)

[17] Murgatroyd, S. (2011) *Six Revolutions and Their Impact*. Presentation given to the Meeting of Fellow of the Royal Society for Arts and Manufacturing, Vancouver in July 2011 available at www.slideshare.com

[18] Murgatroyd, S and Simpson, D (2010) *Renaissance Leadership – Rethinking and Leading the Future*. New York: Lulu Press (www.lulu.com).

[19] See http://www.kff.org/entmedia/upload/8010.pdf (Accessed September 12th 2011)

[20] Veen, W. & Vrakking, B. (2006) *Homo Zappiens: growing up in a digital age.* London, Continuum International Publishing Group

[21] Hargreaves, A et al. *The Learning Mosaic: A Multiple Perspectives Review of the Alberta Initiative for School Improvement (AISI)* (Alberta Education, September 2009).

[22] Stiglitz, J.E. (2006). *Making globalization work* (New York: W W Norton).

[23] Dulchinos, D.P, (2005). *Neurosphere - the convergence of evolution, group mind and the internet* (Boston: Red Wheel / Weiser LLC).

[24] Kurzweil, R. (2005) *The Singularity is Near.* (New York: Viking), 122-142.

[25] Robinson, K. *Do Schools Kill Creativity?* (26 June 2006) <http://www.ted.com/talks/lang/eng/ken_robinson_says_schools_kill_creativity.html> [9 September 2011]

[26] Veen, W. and Vrakking, B. *Homo zappiens: growing up in a digital age* (London: Continuum International Publishing Group, 2006).

[27] Hayes, T and Malone, M.S. *No Size Fits All – From Mass Marketing to Mass Handselling.* (New York: Portfolio Books, 2009).

[28] Tucker, M (2011) *Standing on the Shoulders of Giants: An American Agenda for Educational Reform.* (National Centre on Education and the Economy, May 24th, 2011) (mimeo) at page 39

[29] Sahlberg, Pasi. *Finnish Lessons – What Can the World Learn from Educational Change in Finland.* (Columbia: Teachers College Press, 2011).

Chapter 2

[30] Rogers, E (1962) The Diffusion of Innovations. Glencoe: Free Press.

[31] Alberta Teachers' Association (2009) Looking Forward. Edmonton, Alberta Teachers' Association.

[32] The Guardian (UK). Stress *Drives Teachers Out of Schools*. (25 April 2011) <http://www.guardian.co.uk/education/2011/apr/25/stress-drives-teachers-out-of-schools> [20th August 2011]

[33] Mansell, J. *Deinstitutionalization and Community Living*. (London: Chapman & Hall, 1996)

[34] This is not always the case, however. See Burke, K. *An Accidental Advocate*. (Edmonton: Sexton, 2011).

[35] Gottlieb, L. "How to Land Your Kid in Therapy." *The Atlantic Monthly*. (July|August 2011).

[36] Aris, Sarajane and Murgatroyd, S (2012) Beyond Resilience – Mastery, Meaning-Making and Compassion. Edmonton: Future Think Press.

[37] Source: Statistics Canada

[38] Unemployment in the UK in June 2011 was 2.43 million, in the US 13.9 million, in Canada 1.37 million and across the EU (without the UK) 20.82 million.

[39] Murgatroyd, S "Wicked Problems and the Work of the School." *European Journal of Education* 45, no. 2 (2010): 259-279.

[40] Hines, Barry. *A Kestrel for a Knave*. (London: Penguin, 1968).

[41] *Billy Elliot* written by Lee Hall and directed by Stephen Daldry starring Jamie Bell, Julie Walters, Gary Lewis and Jamie Draven. BBC Productions with Tiger Aspect, Studio Canal and WT[2] Productions. September 29th 2000.

[42] Robinson, K. *Do Schools Kill Creativity?* (26 June 2006) <http://www.ted.com/talks/lang/eng/ken_robinson_says_schools_kill_creativity.html> [9 September 2011]

[43] Robinson, Ken. *RSA Animate – Changing Education Paradigms*. (2011) <http://www.youtube.com/watch?v=zDZFcDGpL4U> [February 18th 2011].

[44] Described more fully in Sahlberg, P (2011) Finnish Lessons. Columbia: Teachers College Press.

[45] See Salhberg, P (2011) op.cit.

[46] There are five levels of literacy. Level 3 is universally regarded as the level required for effective functioning in most workplace settings. The five levels are: **Level 5 –** Very strong skills able to find information in dense text and make high-level inferences or use specialized background information; **Level 4 –** Strong skills able to

integrate and synthesize information from complex or lengthy passages.; **Level 3 – Adequate skills for coping in a complex** advanced society. Equivalent to the skill level required for high school completion and college entry; **Level 2** – Weak skills, can deal with simple clearly laid out material. May be able to cope with everyday demands but will have difficulty with new situations; **Level 1** – Very poor skills, may not be able to determine the correct dosage from the label on a medicine bottle.

Chapter 3

[47] Meyer, M. and Zucker, L. *Permanently failing organizations.* (Newbury Park, CA: Sage, 1998).

[48] Sharkey, M. "Professor David Reynolds offers his views on the small rural school debate." *Western Mail.* (January 1, 2009), p. 2.

[49] Rouleau, L., Gagnon, S., and Clouter, C. "Revisiting permanently-failing organizations - A practice perspective." *Montreal: Les Cahiers de Recherché du GePS* 2(1) (2008), 17-29.

[50] Senge, P. *The fifth discipline - the art and practice of the learning organization.* (New York: Doubleday, 1990).

[51] Senge, P. *The fifth discipline - the art and practice of the learning organization.* (New York: Doubleday, 1990), 387-388)

[52] Bynner, J. "Literacy, numeracy and employability - evidence from the British birth cohort studies." *Literacy & Numeracy Studies* 13(1) (2004), 31 - 48.

[53] Alexander, R. (ed). *Children, their world, their education – final report of the Cambridge primary review.* (London: Routledge, 2009).

[54] See, for example, the focused video presentation at http://www.youtube.com/watch?v=8_ehGLqzBVM [20th Feb 2011] for a critical reflection on these skills.

[55] Robinson, Sir Ken et al. *All Our Futures – Creativity, Culture and Education.* (London: National Advisory Committee on Creative and Cultural Education, 2008).

[56] See, for example, his presentations to the Royal Society for Arts and Manufacturing at http://www.youtube.com/watch?v=zDZFcDGpL4U [February 18th 2011].

[57] Jenson, J., Taylor, N and Fisher, S. *Critical Review and Analysis of the Issue – "Skills, Technology and Learning" Final Report.* (Unpublished manuscript, 2010).

[58] See, for example, a series of White Papers from Pearson documenting their approach to personalized learning: http://www.pearsoned.com/press/2010/10/13/pearsons-new-white-paper-outlines-intervention-models-provides-guidance-for-creating-customized-learning-road-maps.htm [18th Feb 2011].

[59] See, for example, Sahlberg, P. "Education reform for raising economic competitiveness." *Journal of Educational Change*, 7(4) (2006), 259-287

[60] Alberta introduced a new School Act in March 2011 intended to enable the adoption of 21st Century Skills and more closely align the requirements imposed upon schools by the Province with the need for flexibility and nimbleness at the level of the school. Similar changes are also being made in New Brunswick. Finland, in reviewing its school system, is also looking to "rebalance" the curriculum, while Singapore continues its innovations around the policy of "teach less, learn more".

[61] Couture, J.C. and Booi, L (2011) Testing, Testing – What Alberta Can Learn from Finland About Standardization and the Role of the Teacher. Alberta Views, September pages 28-32.

[62] iNet—International Networking for Educational Transformation *What We Do: Our Priorities: Personalising Learning*. (Taunton, Somerset: Specialist Schools and Academies Trust, 2010). <www.ssat- inet.net/whatwedo/personalisinglearning.aspx> [Feb 17th 2011].

[63] Anderson, C.A. "A Neuroscience of Children and Media?" *Journal of Children and Media* 1, no. 1 (2007): 77–85.

[64] Kaiser Family Foundation. *Generation M2: Media in the Lives of 8–18 Year Olds*. (Menlo Park, CA: Henry J. Kaiser Family Foundation, 2010)

[65] Canadian Paediatric Society. *Impact of Media Use on Children and Youth*. (Ottawa, Ontario: Canadian Paediatric Society, 2009). <www.cps.ca/english/statements/CP/pp03-01.htm#RECOMMENDATIONS> [18th Feb 2011].

[66] Dretzin, R. (Producer). (September 22, 2009). "Interview with Sherry Turkle." *Frontline* [Television Broadcast]. Public Broadcasting Station at http://www.pbs.org/wgbh/pages/frontline/digitalnation/learning/concentration/saving-stillness.html?play [Feb 17th, 2011].

[67] MacDonald, E. and Shirley, D. *The Mindful Teacher*. (New York: Teachers College Press, 2009).

[68] Murgatroyd, S. *Wicked Problems and the Work of the School. European Journal of Education*, Volume 45(2), Part 1 (2010): 259-279.

[69] UNESCO (1999) Learning – The Treasure Within. Paris: UNESCO

[70] The description of the four pillars owes a great deal to the text of the UNESCO report, available at http://www.unesco.org/delors/fourpil.htm (Accessed on August 1st 2011).

[71] See note 32 above.

[72] See, for example: Gardner, H. *Intelligence Reframed. Multiple intelligences for the 21st century*, (New York: Basic Books, 1999); and also Gardner, H. *The Disciplined Mind: Beyond Facts And Standardized Tests, The K-12 Education That Every Child Deserves*. (New York: Simon and Schuster [and New York: Penguin Putnam], 1999).

Chapter 4

[73] MacDonald, E. Shirley, D. *The Mindful Teacher.* (New York: Teachers College Press, 2009)

[74] Project SUMIT (2000) *SUMIT Compass Points Practices.*
<http://pzweb.harvard.edu/Research/SUMIT.htm>. [June 15, 2011]

[75] Sahlberg, Pasi. *Finnish Lessons – What Can the World Learn from Educational Change in Finland.* (Columbia: Teachers College Press, 2011). *op.cit.*

[76] Tucker, M (2011) *Standing on the Shoulders of Giants: An American Agenda for Educational Reform.* (National Centre on Education and the Economy, May 24th, 2011) (mimeo).

[77] ibid

[78] A statement made at the 2011 Summit on the Teaching Profession, held by US Education Secretary Arnie Duncan, in New York in March 2011. See Tucker, M (2011), *op.cit* at page 14.

Chapter 5

[79] Tucker, M (2011) op.cit.

[80] Margolis, C. And Buchanan, R. *The idea of design* (Cambridge, MA: MIT Press, 1995).

[81] Margolis, C. And Buchanan, R. *The idea of design* (Cambridge, MA: MIT Press, 1995).

[82] Hara, N. *Communities of practice: fostering peer-to-peer learning and informal knowledge sharing in the work place* (New York: Springer, 2008).

[83] Dini, D. *Game design and technology* (Liverpool: Liverpool John Moores University Workshop on Gaming, 2005).

[84] Gardner, H. *Five minds for the future* (Boston, MA: Harvard University Press, 2006).

[85] Facione, P. (2009, March). *Critical thinking: what it is and why it counts.* Insight Assessment: <http://www.insightassessment.com/pdf_files/what&why2006.pdf> [April 5, 2009].

[86] Murgatroyd, S "Wicked Problems and the Work of the School." *European Journal of Education* 45, no. 2 (2010): 259-279

[87] Asheim, B., Boschma, R., and Cooke, P. "Constructing regional advantage - platform policies based on related variety and differentiated knowledge base." *Papers in Evolutionary Economic Geography (PEEG) from Utrecht University, Section of*

Economic Geography (Utrecht: Utrecht University, Section of Economic Geography, 2007).

[88] Jeffrey, B., and Woods, P. *Creative learning in the primary school.* (London: Taylor & Francis, 2009). ; Sawyer, R.K. "Education for innovation", *Thinking Skills and Creativity*, (2006): 41-48.

[89] Clifford, P., and Marinucci, S.J. "Testing the water: three elements of classroom inquiry." *Harvard Educational Review*, 78(4), (2008): 675-688.

[90] Churchman, C.W. "Wicked problems." *Management Science*, 14(4), (1967): 141-2.

[91] Rittel, H., and Melvin, M. *Dilemmas in a general Theory of planning* (Berkeley California: Institute of Urban and Regional Development, University of California, Berkeley, 1972).

[92] Margolis, C. And Buchanan, R. *The idea of design* (Cambridge, MA: MIT Press, 1995).

[93] Murgatroyd, S "Wicked Problems and the Work of the School." *European Journal of Education* 45, no. 2 (2010): 259-279.

[94] Kirschner, P. A. "Why minimal guidance during instruction does not work - an analysis of the failure of constructivist, discovery, problem-based, experiential, and inquiry based teaching." *Educational Psychologist* 41(2), (2006): 75–86.

[95] Jardine, D.W., Clifford, P., and Friesen, S. *Curriculum in abundance* (New York: Taylor & Francis, 2006);
Jardine, D. W., Clifford, P., Kluth, P. and Friesen, S. *Back to the basics of teaching and learning: thinking the world together* (New York: Taylor & Francis, 2002).

[96] Hmelo-Silver, C.E., G.D.R., and Chinn, C.A. "Scaffolding and achievement in problem-based and inquiry learning." *Educational Psychologist*, 42(2), (2007): 99–107.

[97] Clifford, P., and Marinucci, S.J. "Testing the water: three elements of classroom inquiry." *Harvard Educational Review*, 78(4), (2008): 675-688.

[98] Murgatroyd, S "Wicked Problems and the Work of the School." *European Journal of Education* 45, no. 2 (2010): 259-279.

[99] Clifford, P., Friesen, S. and Jardine, D.W. *Back to the Basics of Teaching and Learning – Thinking the World Together.* (New Jersey: Lawrence Erlbaum & Associates, 2003); Friesen, S. *What Did You Learn in School Today? Teaching Effectiveness – A Framework and a Rubric.* (Toronto: Canadian Education Association, 2009).

[100] Google. *Google Translate.* <http://translate.google.com/translate> [August 19th 2011]

[101] Murgatroyd, S and Couture, J.C. *Using Technology to Support Real Learning First in Alberta Schools.* (Edmonton, AB: The Alberta Teachers' Association, 2010).

[102] The EU has commissioned a range of studies of agents. Sony is working on a major project, the aim of which is the development of a new generation of embodied agents that are able to interact directly (i.e., without human intervention) with the

physical world and to communicate between them and with other agents (including humans). This will be achieved through the development of new design principles, algorithms, and mechanisms that can extend the functionality of existing technological artifacts (mobile phone, WI-FI devices, robots and robot-like artifacts, etc.) and can lead to the development of new artifacts.

[103] See *The Semantic Web: An Introduction* http://infomesh.net/2001/swintro/ [September 9, 2011] See http://www.autonomy.com/

[104] This technology is already in use at the University of Calgary medical school and is being explored by the Northern Ontario School of Medicine. It will be in widespread use by 2012 and related technologies, with low cost, will appear in other fields from 2009 onwards. It makes possible this scenario: a doctor has to operate on an individual's tongue as part of a facial reconstruction due to an accident. The simulation provides the doctor with a precise assessment of the impact of the choices he or she makes on future speech, swallowing and other behaviours which require the tongue — where he or she cuts will impact these things.

[105] Hayes, T and Malone, M.S. *No Size Fits All – From Mass Marketing to Mass Handselling*. (New York: Portfolio Books, 2009).

[106] See Honda's work on ASIMO at http://world.honda.com/ASIMO/ and see also Sony's work at http://web.csl.sony.fr/Research/Topics/DevelopmentalRobotics/

[107] For a review of the most recent developments here, see http://web.nature.com/nature/journal/v440/n7083/full/440409a.html

[108] Kurzweil, R. (2005) *The Singularity is Near*. (New York: Viking), 122-142.

[109] Thought based computing is now being displayed at several computer trade shows — see <http://www.mg.co.za/articlepage.aspx?area=/breaking_news/breaking_news__international_news/&articleid=265991> for an example from Germany.

[110] A great deal of this section appeared in Murgatroyd, S. and Couture, J.C. *Using Technology to Support Real Learning First in Alberta Schools*. (Edmonton, AB: The Alberta Teachers' Association, 2010). It is used here with full acknowledgement.

[111] This chapter makes no reference to the important role of faculty in basic research and in community service. It focuses solely on their teaching role. This is not intended to denigrate these other roles; it is simply a matter of focus.

[112] Clifford, P., Friesen, S. and Jardine, D.W. *Back to the Basics of Teaching and Learning – Thinking the World Together*. (New Jersey: Lawrence Erlbaum & Associates, 2003).

[113] Looker, E D and V Thiessen. "Beyond the Digital Divide in Canadian Schools." *Social Science Comprehensive Review* (2009):475–90.; Selwyn, N. "Reconsidering Political and Popular Understandings of the Digital Divide." *New Media Society 6* (2004): 341–62.; Sciadas, G. *The Digital Divide in Canada*. (Ottawa: Statistics Canada, 2000)

[114] Organisation for Economic Co-operation and Development (May 2008). *New Millennium Learners: Initial Findings on the Effects of Digital Technologies on School-Age Learners*. Centre for Educational Research and Innovation (CERI). < www.oecd.org/dataoecd/39/51/40554230.pdf.>

[115] For more information, see www.nectac.org/topics/atech/udl.asp.

[116] Alberta Teachers' Association. *Looking Forward*. (Edmonton, Alta: Author, 2009).

[117] Hargreaves, A. and Shirley, D. *The Fourth Way: The Inspiring Future for Educational Change*. (Thousand Oaks, California: Corwin Press, 2009)

[118] Hargreaves, A. and Shirley, D. *The Fourth Way: The Inspiring Future for Educational Change*. (Thousand Oaks, California: Corwin Press, 2009)

[119] McRae, P. and Parsons, J. "A Longitudinal Study on Technology Integration Initiatives and the Complexities of Research Partnerships Across Organizational Borders." In Reeves, T., and Yamashita, S. (eds), *Proceedings of World Conference on E-Learning in Corporate, Government, Healthcare, and Higher Education* (Chesapeake, Va: American Association for the Advancement of Computing in Education (AACE,) 2006): 757–62. /See McKay, N (2008) at page 8. Who is McKay?

[120] Hargreaves, A. and Fink, D. *Sustainable Leadership*. (San Francisco: Jossey-Bass, 2006).

[121] Collins, J. *Good to Great*. (New York: Random House, 2001); Broughton, P.D. *Ahead of the Curve*. (New York: Penguin Press, 2008)

[122] Friesen, S. *What Did You Do in School Today? Teaching Effectiveness—A Framework and Rubric*. (Ottawa: Canadian Educational Association, 2009).

[123] (Wiliam et al 2004

[124] Gilbert, J. *Catching the Knowledge Wave—The Knowledge Society and the Future of Education*. (Wellington, New Zealand: NZCER Press, 2005).

[125] From http://www.pearsoned.com/pr_2009/072109.htm [December 11th, 2010] – describing a publication, Personalized Learning: The Nexus of 21st Century Learning and Educational Technologies.

[126] Source: Ambient Insight Industry Analysis of e-Learning, 2011.

Chapter 6

[127] I am grateful to my colleague and friend, Dr Phil McRae of the Alberta Teachers' Association, who published an article on personalized learning in the ATA Magazine. See McRae, P. (2010) "The Politics of Personalization." *ATA Magazine, Fall* (Edmonton: Alberta Teachers' Association, 2010)

[128] Hargreaves, D. *Personalising Learning: Next Steps in Working Laterally*. (London: Specialist Schools and Academies Trust, 2004) - also cited in McRae, *op cit.*

[129] Hargreaves, D. *Personalising Learning 6: The Final Gateway: School Design and Organisation.* (London: Specialist Schools and Academies Trust, 2006) - also cited in McRae, *op cit.*

[130] Hargreaves, A. and Shirley, D. *The Fourth Way: The Inspiring Future for Educational Change.* (Thousand Oaks, California: Corwin Press, 2009)- also cited in McRae, *op cit.*

[131] Fullan, M. (2009) *Michael Fullan's Answer to "What is Personalized Learning?"* Microsoft Education Partner Network. See http://en.wikipedia.org/wiki/Personalized_learning (Accessed on 27th September 2011) [August 18, 2011] - also cited in MacRae, *op cit.*

[132] This suggesting came from the Challenge Dialogue Paper prepared for the symposium *What Makes a Great School?* See http://www.learningourway.ca/index.php/our-schools-r

[133] Universities in Finland accept applicants who have graduated from high school or upper secondary school with an IB (International Baccalaureate), EB (European Baccalaureate) or Reifeprüfung diploma (in any country offering these type of qualifications) or with a Finnish Upper Secondary School Diploma in English.

[134] Sahlberg, Pasi. *Finnish Lessons – What Can the World Learn from Educational Change in Finland.* (Columbia: Teachers College Press, 2011). *op cit.*

[135] Murgatroyd, S and Henry, N. *Schools, Accountability and Performance – A Challenge Paper.* (Edmonton, AB: Alberta Teacher Association, 2007). This paper was focused on the accountability pillar in Alberta. In this chapter, I have extended this analysis to cover different accountability systems which are similar in intent and design to the Alberta model.

[136] See Murgatroyd, S. "Managing for Performance – Quality, Accreditation and Assessment in Distance Education." In Evans, T., Haughey, M., and Murphy, D. [eds.] *International Handbook of Distance Education.* (Bingley, UK: Emerald Group Publishing, 2008): 567-584

[137] Hargreaves, A. and Shirley, D. *The Fourth Way: The Inspiring Future for Educational Change.* (Thousand Oaks, California: Corwin Press, 2009)

[138] Giddens, A. *The Third Way – The Renewal of Social Democracy.* (Malden, MA: Blackwell, 1999)

[139] MacDonald, E., and Shirley, D. *The Mindful Teacher.* (New York: Teachers College Press, 2009).

[140] An account of the development of accountability in education in Alberta is given by McEwan, N. "Educational Accountability in Alberta." *Canadian Journal of Education*, Volume 20(1) (1995): 27-44.

[141] David King cited in *Real Learning First – The Teaching Professions View of Student Assessment, Evaluation and Accountability for the 21st Century.* (Edmonton, AB: Alberta Teachers' Association): 15.

[142] New Brunswick has adopted an approach to twenty first century skills and learning but wishes to strengthen its high stakes testing regime. See *NB3-21C: Creating a 21st Century Learning Model of Public Education Three-Year Plan 2010-2013* at http://www.district6.nbed.nb.ca/PDF/NB3-21Cconsultationdocument2nd2edition.pdf (Accessed on 27th September 2011) [June 12th 2010] especially at pages 26 and 32-33.

[143] See, for example, Reynolds, D.R., Sullivan, M. and Murgatroyd, S. *The Comprehensive Experiment – A Comparison of the Selective and Non Selective System of School Organization.* (Lewes: Falmer Press, 1987); and also Reynolds, D. et al. *Bringing Schools Back In.* (Lewes: Falmer Press, 1987); as well as Rutter, M. et al. *Fifteen Thousand Hours.* (London: Open Books, 1979).

[144] Based in parts on developments in Ireland, see <http://www.sdpi.ie/> [July 3rd 2010].

[145] Davies, B. and Ellison, L. *Strategic Direction and Development of the School: Key Frameworks for School Improvement Planning.* (New York: Routledge-Falmer, 2003).

[146] Murgatroyd, S. and Morgan, C. *Total Quality Management and the School.* (Milton Keynes: The Open University Press, 1992)

[147] The ATA is very clear that this is an optional use of personal improvement plans – teachers are free to pursue other interests, such as curriculum related, skills development of graduate studies.

[148] Deming, W. E. *Quality, Productivity and Competitive Position.* (Boston: MIT Press, 1982)

[149] Murgatroyd, S. and Simpson, D (2010) *Renaissance Leadership – Rethinking and Leading the Future.* New York: Lulu Press.

[150] Murgatroyd, S. and Simpson, D (2010) *Renaissance Leadership – Rethinking and Leading the Future.* New York: Lulu Press.

[151] Carver, John. "Remaking Governance." *American School Board Journal* (March 2000): 26—30. ED 536 841

[152] Dawson, L,J., and Quinn, R. "Clarifying Board and Superintendent Roles." *The School Administrator* (March, 2000): 12—14, 18. ED 636 863

[153] Moscovitch, R., Sadovnik, A., et al *Governance and Urban School Improvement – Lessons for New Jersey from Nine Cities.* (New York: The Institute for Education Law and Policy, Rutgers University, 2009) (mimeo). Available at <http://ielp.rutgers.edu/docs/MC%20Final.pdf> [20th August 2011].

[154] Viteritti, J [editor] *When Mayors Take Charge: School Governance in the City.* (Washington, DC: The Brookings Institute, 2009): 9

[155] Moscovitch, R., Sadovnik, A., et al *Governance and Urban School Improvement – Lessons for New Jersey from Nine Cities.* (New York: The Institute for Education Law and Policy, Rutgers University, 2009) (mimeo). Available at <http://ielp.rutgers.edu/docs/MC%20Final.pdf> [20th August 2011].

[156] In fact, Alberta has 304 educational authorities. 41 public school boards, 17 separate boards, 5 francophone school systems, 13 charter school authorities, 102 ECS Private authorities and 126 private schools. In total, there are 2,140 schools in Alberta.

[157] Murgatroyd, S. and Morgan, C (1992) *Total Quality Management and the School*. Milton Keynes: Open University Press.